Building a Business Building a Life

A Memoir & Workbook

by Karen Lorene

© 2011 Lorene Publications

All Rights Reserved. No portion of this publication may be reproduced or transmitted in any form by any means, electronic or mechanical, without permission in writing from the publisher.

Lorene Publications
1420 Fifth Avenue, Suite 108, Seattle, WA 98101
lorenepublications.com

The Blurb-provided layout designs and graphic elements are copyright Blurb Inc., 2011. This book was created using the Blurb creative publishing service. The book author retains sole copyright to his or her contributions to this book.

blurb.com

CONTENTS

Introduction	5
Ch. 1 - In the Beginning	12
Ch. 2 - Baby Steps and Giant Steps	17
Ch. 3 - This Wasn't in Any Business Plan	23
Ch. 4 - Moving On	31
Ch. 5 - Surviving a Stalker	40
Ch. 6 - When the Right One	54
Ch. 7 - Thinking Big, Then Bigger	60
Ch. 8 - Giving a Party	70
Ch. 9 - Falling in Love with a Space	76
Ch. 10 - A Knight in Shining Armor	82
Ch. 11 - I Think I'll Slit My Wrists	90
Ch. 12 - Who Wears This Stuff?	104
Ch. 13 - Antiques Roadshow	113
Ch. 14 - The Writing Business	124
Ch. 15 - Stayin' Alive, Stayin' Alive	129
Ch. 16 - Artists	136
Ch. 17 - Customers and a Bit More	141
Ch. 18 - Rant and Rave	151
Ch. 19 - Pay Attention	158
Postscript - Twice and Thrice Told Tales	161
Workbook Chapters 1-19	179-291

Building A Business, Building A Life

This book is dedicated to all of the employees
who have helped build this business.

Barbara Doldge
Lysa Hanson
Lael Hagan
Diane Hagan
Tammy Holt
Jim Morgan
Randall Bullo
Virginia Washburn
Jeanne Eaton
Kim Zirbes
Ruth Ellen Elliott
Dana Shaw
Mary Clare Thompson
Jill Green
Helen Brooks
Ellen de Groot
Susan G. Welch
Lorraine Vagner
Nadine Kariya
Mēgan Corwin
Trudee Hill

Special thanks to Sue Jostrom, editor; Trudee Hill, designer; Don Bell, reader/listener; Stephen Fletcher, business consultant; Priscilla Long, teacher; and to all the members of Super Group who for sixteen years have read and critiqued most of these words.

INTRODUCTION

In my first year of high school, I envied Sandra. While the rest of us in the freshmen class were practicing how to shape our lips into perfect bows with Bubble-Gum-Pink lipstick, Sandra had, as my mother said, "blossomed." There wasn't much to do about one's blossoms except wait. But, not only had Sandra blossomed, she wore long, gorgeous necklaces: chains with stones and faceted glass baubles. I imagined she had dozens and dozens of necklaces, so seen by my envious eyes, but she certainly had three. I remember thinking *when I grow up, I will have necklaces*. That thought lay dormant and hidden. It has crossed my mind that had I not sat three rows behind Sandra all year, admiring the back of her perfectly coiffed hair and the glint of each necklace closure, I might not now be the owner of Facèré Jewelry Art Gallery.

How did I get from envy to fulfillment in the world of jewelry? My very first rush of pure jewelry satisfaction came at my sixteenth birthday dinner. My parents watched with great expectation as I unwrapped the "important" present (less important presents which arrived at the bottom of our beds on our birthday morning had already been opened). The major gift came at dinner. Wrapped and bowed in bright silver foil, my parents watched as I opened the tiny ring box. A glint of green. A four stone, emerald ring! How glorious! How grown-up! I wore it with pride. The ring was my grandmother's and of all her many grandchildren, I was the lucky person on which it was bestowed.

And so I wore my ring: full of history and status and love.

And then? In 1984, at a week-long gemology course at the Gemological Institute of America in Santa Monica I learned to use a refractometer. I dabbed the tiniest amount of fluid on the crystal in the center of the refractometer and gently lowered the center stone of my emerald ring to take a reading. The index should have read 1.577. I tried again. And again. No matter how many times I turned the stone and reapplied the fluid the index read 1.44. I did not give up easily, but when I did, I knew these emeralds were glass.

I never told my parents. As soon as I could afford them, I bought four fine emeralds and had them set. I never, ever mentioned this trickery to my parents and never ever challenged the story about how Grandpa had to paint six houses to earn enough money to pay for Grandma's very special, very precious, emerald ring.

On my right hand I wore my late-Victorian gold and emerald ring. On my left hand I wore my wedding band. Perfect. A ring for each hand. And today? A few more rings. Eleven in all.

It never crossed my mind that too many rings might be perceived as frivolous, shameful, questionable, or in any way, unbecoming. For instance, as I settled into the business of jewelry, should it not have occurred to me that customers should be spending money on children who need dental care, or on criminals who need half-way houses, or on women who need shelters? Was I not appalled at Elizabeth Taylor and all of her flaunted wealth? Appalled at rappers with two-carat diamonds in their ears? Was I in no way disconcerted by my neighbor's daughter, who, when coming to occupy a chair next to me would cross her legs and then cross her hands on top of her knee, her left hand on top, to once again let me see her bounteous diamond?

Well, sure. I am aware of the contradictions that surround jewelry. And yet I know for certain that in some mysterious way, the human species requires adornment and has since the beginning of time. Proof surrounds us. Think of the strange jewelry finds; one of the oldest in history is in France at Arcy-sur-Cure. Thirty-one thousand years old. A necklace of marmot, fox, wolf and hyena teeth.

I have read with awe about The English Fishpool Hoard from the 1300s found in 1966 which offered up gold coins, gold rings, and gold chain

Or consider The Nuestra Senora de Atocha from 1622, found in 1985 in the Florida Keys. It revealed 40 tons of gold, copper, silver, and emeralds along with the most awe inspiring four-inch gold cross set with the purest of emeralds.

The history of sunken treasure never ceases to fascinate. The list goes on and there is not a *National Geographic* that does not draw one's attention to such discoveries. One I remember most was the 1985 discovery in Stroda Sloska, Poland. Page after page of golden treasures—one of the most important finds in the twentieth century. What excitement and glory came to those archaeologists who brought up from the ground a gold crown, four gold pendants, a medieval clasp decorated with gemstones, a ring with the heads of dragons, a sapphire ring, and the most exquisite—a ring with a moon and stars?

Stranger still are the jewelry finds buried with bodies. Crowns, and toe rings, and labrets. A whole history of jewelry prepared to adorn the wearer in the after-life (although it crosses my mind, that perhaps the buried artifacts were for bribing St. Peter at the Golden Gate).

In May of 2010, my husband, Don, and I watched at the home of Shakespeare in Stratford, student archaeologists sift through a four-foot by four-foot by two-inch square of dirt. They found a single bead! Great excitement surrounded that discovery. The honorable bead was carried inside to be placed with metal bits and strings and broken pottery.

Is all of this interest in jewelry to be questioned? Indeed.

Think of the poor. Think of the needy. There are days it is difficult to live with my ambiguity over the lush, over-done, too much jewelry of the past and present.

Would Sister Teresa have found the world's interest, fascination, accumulation of jewelry worthy of confession? Or, consider all the Popes through time. They more than likely have had no troubled thoughts about adornment.

Or is it possible that St. Francis of Assisi considered the birds that came to rest on his shoulders—a form of adornment?

The confusion, my confusion, surrounding jewelry is perhaps no more or no less than the confusion that comes with being human. There are times when I'm busy managing the gallery, I let the thoughts of blood diamonds and slave labor and the fact that I should be helping the poor slip away. I accept the fact that I am helping others—fifty jewelry artists. I help them find their dream. There is not one jeweler I work with who has not said in so many words, "I picked up the torch and I knew, I just knew, this was what I wanted to do for the rest of my life!" My job? To continue to find customers for their creations. For their sake and mine, I convince others to adorn their bodies. And I do my share.

Besides my eleven rings, I have in my home a "bracelet wall." On an opposite wall I have three wooden racks that hold my necklaces Extra rings are grouped on a miniature hat rack. Earrings are tucked into boxes with wooden separators.

Too many? Too much? When excess crosses my mind, I bundle up pieces and give them to my favorite charity auctions. I make room for the inevitable next piece.

I have favorite pieces. Don purchased two spectacular pieces of jewelry for me... "Spectacular" means the ring and the pin he gifted me are exactly right and exactly sentimental. The first piece of jewelry Don secretly commissioned was a pin the size and construction of a sorority pin, except my pin is: a miniature clipboard attached by a gold chain to a diamond embedded whistle. On the clipboard are the words, "Everyone out in the street for volleyball." This piece speaks to two sentiments: it commemorates the movie we saw, *A Thousand Clowns*, the night we decided to marry. Jason Robards yells those words out a window down an empty street. The scene is forever in my memory. The other sentiment is directed toward my bossy, organizing side which I believe he respects and disparages with equal vigor. The second piece of jewelry he had made for me is a band with twenty tiny diamonds, for our twentieth anniversary—a perfect surprise.

If the house were robbed, those two pieces, plus my mother's tiniest diamond filled wedding band, would be my greatest losses. But then, I'd hate to lose my "street-sweeper" ring made from the bristles of an actual street sweeper. And I do have quite a nice diamond ring in platinum from the 1920s. I'm quite fond of it. It does not, however, in any way outweigh the stainless-steel ring that holds the tiniest of diamonds in a crack that runs across the ring and fondly reminds me of Leonard Cohen's beautiful poem, "…there's a crack in everything, that's how the light gets in." Oh, yes, and recently I added an 1890s carved moonstone. That makes the eleventh ring. There is something satisfying about that number, if for no other reason than it makes me hear my mother's voice saying, "…too many rings and you will look like a woman of the streets!" Those words make me smile.

Jewelry comes and goes. I left a fabulous antique pansy pin on a suit that went to the cleaners and never came back. I yearned for a piece of jewelry in another store for over a year and was devastated when one day I went to reconsider it for the hundredth time and it was gone. Sold! I miss it to this day.

And robbery? I've not been robbed. I always

think that a robber would look at my collection and wonder why anyone would want it. Plastic and acrylic and street-sweeper bristles. The crook would never understand.

When I hear of jewelry being stolen, my heart breaks for those customers. Any loss of jewelry tears at one's heart. If you have had jewelry stolen, you know the loss. For those of you who doubt the joy of adornment and the confusion and pain of loss, let me quote to you from an article that recently appeared in the *Seattle Times*. The article concerned a home-break-in. Officer Ferrell had this to say: "It (jewelry) is what we carry through generations, and has great connection to our lives; it is stuff that is heartbreaking when it is lost."

I couldn't have said it better myself.

Karen Lorene

CHAPTER ONE
IN THE BEGINNING

The University of Chicago Laboratory School

Business skills? Certainly not immediately apparent.

My employable skills were those of a grade school teacher. I had taught elementary from the winter of 1984 through summer of 1991. I taught third grade in a private school, fourth grade in a public school, kindergarten in Chicago's south side, and third and fourth grades at The University of Chicago Laboratory School.

In 1896 John Dewey founded The Lab School. That school grew from the principle of hands-on

Building A Business, Building A Life

learning and exploration. Dewey's philosophy came to fruition in a building he designed next to the Midway in Hyde Park, Illinois. Generous windows spilled light into spacious rooms. Tables and chairs were not attached to the floor and could be moved and rearranged at will. Science was taught in rooms equipped for experimentation. Play areas were provided indoors and out. A large library contained quantities of books available for touching, perusing, and reading.

The teachers at The Lab School recognized that children learn in different ways at different speeds with different learning capabilities. Teachers embraced Dewey's philosophy. The Laboratory School was an incubator for learning and both teachers and students were constantly examining, changing, analyzing, and evaluating how knowledge was absorbed.

Grounded in Dewey's philosophy, I filled room 204 with microscopes and an ant farm; dictionaries, novels, and biographies; tape recorders and books-on-tape; maps, encyclopedias and a globe; new-math books, workbooks, and work cards; paints, pastels, crayons, and easels. My students and I converted a closet into a projection room. Around the classroom were areas called "stations" filled with stuff: toys, puzzles, broken appliances, parts of a hand-set printer, nuts and bolts, hammers and nails, wrenches, screwdrivers, calipers, wooden rods for math, boxes of word games, books from the library. The stations changed regularly, but were grounded in developing reading skills, math skills, and social skills.

The children were free to choose what to learn

and when—with the caveat that they were to visit at least five stations a day and keep a written record of their work. Learning happened at each individual's pace, based on interests.

Every child had individual consultations. Each reported his or her accomplishments and I encouraged the students to delve ever more deeply into the subjects that interested them most.

At the end of the year the State of Illinois Standardized Tests proved Dewey right. The children excelled.

I loved being a teacher, but after seven years of teaching, I was ready to enroll in graduate school at the University of Washington. I'd become a teacher of teachers. I was full of ideas and ideals.

Except. Graduate school wasn't what I expected. Professors droned and spoke of children they hadn't seen in twenty years. I changed from one class to another, never finding the joy and excitement I had experienced in the classroom. One day I left campus and didn't return.

The year I quit graduate school, 1971, was also the year teaching positions in the Seattle area disappeared.

I needed employment. I needed an income. I needed a challenge. Why not start a business?

Setting up a business when you know nothing has some advantages. Mistakes are memories before you realize you've made them. Anything and everything seems possible!

On a trip to Spokane, Washington, an opportunity arose. The opportunity resided in my

Building A Business, Building A Life

parents' attic.

"Why would you want that junk?" mom asked.

"I think I'll start an antique business," I said.

"Be my guest," she answered, pleased to be rid of a lot of useless stuff.

I can see what you are imagining. The magical attic. Believe me, mom's attic was not like a calendar picture. It was not full of antiques. It wasn't a treasure trove. It was a small space full of the discards of some thirty years. Nothing had much value. Except for one trunk. That trunk—leather strapped, press-tin-roofed, with wooden stays, had been my grandmother's gift to my dad. That trunk became the touchstone by which I learned to measure the age, quality, value, and importance of the merchandise I began to acquire.

Here's what else was in the attic:

> 1. A rocking chair (not a Windsor, not a prairie-style, not a shaker-type, not much of anything, just a thirty-year-old rocker which needed a new seat)
> 2. Six wooden frames (ornate to plain) and twenty copies of Life Magazine, 1948-1958
> 3. A mahogany side table/magazine holder with coffee-cup stains
> 4. Doilies crocheted by my grandmother
> 5. Six or seven wooden kitchen utensils
> 6. A cross-cut saw

That was it. Thank goodness for the trunk.

Once I started packing the antique trunk, mom scurried around the house finding more items she wouldn't have to take to the Goodwill: a waffle iron with a broken handle, wooden clothes pins in a cross-stitched cloth bag, a washboard and a copper kettle. I piled everything into the van and headed home to Seattle.

I was ecstatic! I had begun a new career.

On the drive home, about the time I crossed the Columbia River into Vantage, I had listed each item in the van and had assigned prices to all but the tin-topped trunk. Most items seemed to me to be worth about ten dollars (small items) and thirty dollars (larger items).

But how much for that gorgeous, turn-of-the-century trunk? Driving home, between Vantage and Ellensburg, the price for the trunk grew from $50 to $120. By the top of Snoqualmie Summit the price grew to $160. By North Bend, $180 seemed more appropriate. By the time I turned into our driveway at home, I decided on the largest sum of money that only the richest person in the world might consider: $200!

It wouldn't be the last time I was wrong.

CHAPTER TWO
BABY STEPS AND GIANT STEPS

Twenty-five stairs to the front door!

The Dewey philosophy left something to be desired when I began my business. The philosophy didn't work well with prospective employees (*let me know if this job sounds interesting*), prospective buyers (*let me know when you need assistance*), prospective bankers (*I'm not quite sure how much I'll need, let me think on it*).

Quickly I learned to ask, and ask with planning and foresight. Sentences changed form and substance:

Here's the job description, I need an answer by the end of the week.

This necklace is the perfect choice for your wife, believe me.

Yes, I need a line of credit. Can you increase it from $10,000 to $15,000? (The next year I asked for $50,000.)

But I'm ahead of myself. I said none of those sentences until I had made my first major mistake. An expensive mistake.

My husband and I rented a house in the Magnolia area of Seattle. The renting agent assured us that the big old house, reminiscent of a Midwest farmhouse, was zoned for commercial purposes. We could live upstairs. The antique shop would be downstairs. A large front porch welcomed customers. I ignored the twenty-five steps one had to climb to get to the front door.

I chose a May spring day in 1972 to open. I arranged merchandise into vignettes as if the customer might walk into someone's home and see an abundance of turn-of-the-century furnishings. I invited everyone I knew for an Open House.

The party was a great success. All my teaching friends attended. Everyone from my husband's office attended. Old and new friends attended. We made two sales: $125 for an oak highchair that folded into a stroller and $10 for a crock filled with blue hydrangeas. We were in the money!

Success? No, disaster.

The morning after our grand opening, the doorbell rang. I was home alone waiting for customers. I hurried to open the door. There stood a man in a suit with a clipboard in his hand. He was not a customer. He was not friendly. He asked me my name. He handed me an envelope. He said, "You're out of compliance with city code. You have to close down."

He was in no way impressed that I had spent my

entire retirement on merchandise. He was not impressed by my pleading. He didn't blink at my tears.

His parting words? "Close it! Now!"

"But this is my business!" I said and gestured as if my arms would embrace the dough table and the butter churn, the wooden rake and the slightly wilted yellow daisies in a metal milk can.

"Sorry, lady. You're zoned residential. Period. No businesses allowed!" He stomped down the porch and almost missed the last step to the sidewalk. He turned to yell, "You need a handrail! Business or not!"

I called my husband in tears and then I went to bed. I had no job. I had no business. I had no location. I slept. I slept sixteen hours. The next day I didn't get out of bed. I couldn't get enough sleep. I was exhausted every day, all day. It was only when *TIME* magazine had a front page article on depression, the major symptom being one of sleeping sixteen hours a day, did I realize I wasn't just tired. I was depressed. It embarrassed me to be diagnosed by a magazine. I got up and out of bed. I cut out the commercial real estate ads. I got in my car. I drove. I needed a location. I needed a business.

Action wiped out depression.

I drove from one side of Seattle to the other. Up and down hills. Through business districts. I looked everywhere. (Remember, there were no computer listings, there were no computers. There was no Craig's List.) What there was was a free paper called *The Little Nickel Ads*. In addition, there was the *Seattle Times* and the *Seattle Post Intelligencer*. I circled every possible location. I drove and drove and drove.

Miracles happen! I found this sign: FOR LEASE. RETAIL SPACES. PIER 70.

Pier 70, on Seattle's waterfront, was in the middle of a total renovation. It was one of the very first projects in Seattle to accommodate small retail businesses. I called. I got an appointment. I didn't know then, but learned later that they were as in need of the first tenants as I was in need of a space. I met with the owner, Edward Dunn, the loveliest of gentlemen with a miniature pink rose in his lapel. I met with the architect, Bud Schorr. Hyper and brilliant. They liked my idea for a turn-of-the-century collectables shop. Mostly they needed names on leases.

I got a lease. I was back in business.

Construction time at Pier 70 gave me time to build an inventory. It wasn't long before my parents were caught up in the business idea. They continued to find furniture, but not just furniture. They found linens and toys and porcelains. They found lamps and cut glass and jewelry. Neighbors and friends had stuff galore. Dad called to tell me that Charlie, the guy across the alley, had a claw-foot table with a missing foot. Would I be able to pay seventy-five dollars for it? Dad assured me he could carve a new foot. I said yes! By now I knew round-oak tables were selling for four hundred dollars. Mom took the phone from dad to say Mrs. Emerson was remodeling her kitchen and would gladly sell her pine dough table, but she wanted ten dollars. Was that okay? Well, sure! How soon could I drive the van back over? Immediately.

My parents loved the fact that they'd be seeing their daughter at least twice a month.

Building A Business, Building A Life

Dad and Mom filled their garage and the spare bedroom. Then the attic. Then the basement. My parents were depression era folks with a panoply of survival skills. There wasn't anything they couldn't refinish or restore. With the packing of each van load they gave me a bill for the items plus ten percent. Looking back, I doubt if the ten percent even covered supplies for refinishing. Make no mistake. I was subsidized.

Everything seemed to be falling into place. What else? I had merchandise. I had a cigar box for money (shades of the childhood lemonade stand). I had a three-ring binder for inventory. I changed the address on my Construction paper cards and printed one hundred. Certainly enough.

I visited stores I liked and tried to see what made them appealing (for instance, Miller-Pollard had vases of paper zinnias, an idea I stole without shame). When Pier 70 opened I filled North Country Fair with the same paper zinnias in vibrant shades of cobalt, wine red, and burnt orange. The brilliant colors played off the oiled oak and stripped pine.

I opened a checking account. I hired an accountant. I asked a girlfriend to work part-time. I began a prospective customer list. That about covered the bases.

North Country Fair opened on November 17, 1972. We sold half of our stock the first month. I drove to Spokane. Customers learned to meet the truck as we unloaded assured they'd get great prices because I hadn't had time to actually look at basic costs or do that very retail thing of "studying the market."

Was I successful? If I could pay to ski, to attend the theatre, to pay the rent on time, then the business must have been successful.

I stumbled and fumbled my way through the first year. From all appearances I was a success. Later I'd learn the truth, but for the moment I had second-hand skis, a season's pass at Snoqualmie, and tickets to The Empty Space Theatre. Life was good!

CHAPTER THREE
THIS WASN'T IN ANY BUSINESS PLAN

Pier 70

Business was good. Sales increased. I opened a second space at Pier 70. Downstairs at North Country Fair I sold collectables (lots of oak, lots of turn-of-the-century stuff) and in the new upstairs shop, Vanity Fair, I sold fine antiques.

Good was followed by better. Richard and Larry, the owners of The Smuggler Restaurant, adjacent to North Country Fair, came by one day and made an offer: "We'd like to buy your space. We need to expand the bar and we're willing to make it worth your while. Think it over and give us an answer by next Tuesday." Amazing! The proposition had the feeling of—*an offer you can't refuse*— with none of the negatives. The owners of the restaurant had become good business friends as we visited outside our front doors waiting for customers to arrive. Lately, however, both of our businesses kept us busy and we'd seen less of each other. Their offer was a great surprise!

I didn't know then, as I know now, that it is rare for someone, anyone, anytime, to offer to buy a small business. And the great thing about this offer was that Richard and Larry didn't want my business. They wanted the space. I hurried home to tell Bruce, my husband, the amazing news.

Bruce had been supportive of my business over those start-up years. He listened. He made suggestions. He drove the van to Spokane. His world was social services. North Country Fair was mine to sell. However, it seemed logical and appropriate to include him in the decision of whether or not to sell.

Neither of us knew anything about selling a business. We didn't know enough to get good advice. In hindsight, what drove the decision were the drives to Spokane. Bruce had come to hate the trips. Selling the store would reduce the need for large items. I could concentrate on "smalls" and reduce the trips to Spokane to three or four times a year. Naively, we never discussed the numbers: profit, loss, cash flow—the logical determinants for selling a business.

Having agreed upon the decision to sell, I went about thinking up the largest possible selling price. The price was determined by looking at how much I owed my parents. To that amount I added two thousand dollars to make me feel good. The next day—I didn't

Building A Business, Building A Life

wait until the next Tuesday—I told the guys I wanted seventeen thousand dollars. They cut the check that afternoon. Was I stupid? Were they generous? It has been almost forty years since the moment Larry handed me that check and it still seems like a lot of money.

With the bill to my parents paid, I made a great decision. I would treat us to a trip to Europe! It was a perfect reward. We took the typical three week, a dozen countries, trip.

How is it that a window opens and a window closes? Given the sale of the shop, the trip to Europe, our bills paid, shouldn't life have been Good! Better! Best? No, life became Good, Better, Bad. I learned my husband was on the verge of an affair.

Words flew. Tears fell. He moved out.

At the advice of a solicitous friend, I wrote down the name of Phyllis Johnson. As my friend declared, "The toughest, meanest, best divorce attorney in Seattle."

I didn't think I'd ever need her name. I thought my husband and I would get back together. What were vows for if they weren't forever? I decided to give him a year. He'd certainly come to his senses.

Summer came and went, and on a beautiful, clear fall day, I sat at the counter in Vanity Fair writing thank-you notes. Light streamed off Puget Sound across the shining hardwood floors and the Plexiglas cases. The gallery brimmed with antique porcelain, crystal, sterling, jewelry, rare books. I stopped mid-task to ruminate on how life wasn't so bad. No question, it would be better when the call came from my estranged husband to admit his mistake and, of course, beg forgiveness.

But the phone didn't ring. I did books. Wiped cases. Polished silver. Stayed busy waiting for customers.

In walked the wife of a prominent member of the non-profit board for which my husband was the executive director. "Hi!" she called as she swept in, breezy with excitement. The woman was short, stocky and sure. She wore Oxford-style, brown walking shoes. A magenta scarf and teal beads wound across her ample front. Her pace and the forward thrust of her bosom made her appear to be a woman on a mission.

I immediately thought to show her the amethyst ring that would go with her outfit. I came from behind the counter to give her a hug hello and guide her to the ring case. Instead, she held me at arms length and said, "You've lost weight. Turn around. My, my you are looking slender and fit! The single life is certainly doing wonders for you!" She stopped, leaned in close and in a semi-whisper, as if someone else might hear, she asked, "Are you alone?"

With a wave of my hand, I indicated we were the only two, and she said with enthusiasm, "Do I have news for you!"

She was close enough that the funereal smell of White Shoulders caught in the back of my throat.

She took a deep breath and reached for my hand. Her eyes locked with mine. She said, "I want to be the first to tell you." She hesitated, the perfect hesitation, and then bit off the words, "It's about your husband."

Building A Business, Building A Life

She hesitated again. "His girlfriend is pregnant."

Through a blur, a buzz, a broken heart, the word 'pregnant' fell in my gut like a boulder. She had to be wrong! I was still married to him. He was going to return and I would be the one to become pregnant.

"Are you okay?" she asked.

I was not okay. She didn't notice. She didn't stop talking.

"I'm sure you want to know how I know. Well, it's no secret! We had a board event the other night, and there he was. With her. Like you didn't exist. I couldn't believe it. She's showing. Like a basketball. He introduced her as if everyone thought it was fine. I don't know what this world is coming to!"

Totally unaware that I needed to sit down. That I needed to throw-up. That tears were seconds away, she grabbed my hand, squeezed my fingers, and leaned to give me a quick kiss on the cheek. "I didn't want just anyone breaking the news." She stepped back to look at me.

Why couldn't she see that I was dying?

"Sweetie, you'll be just fine. Probably better off without him. He hasn't the sense the good Lord gave him. I wasn't the only one who was shocked. You should have heard the chatter in the ladies room. It was the talk of the evening. Shameful. Simply shameful."

She adjusted the scarf around her neck. The beads clattered. Echoed. With my hands behind me, I held on to the counter. I nodded my head as if I agreed.

"I hate to be the bringer of bad news! But it's really not bad news. Everyone thinks you should get on with your life! You should have divorced him months ago. Absolutely months ago!"

She patted my arm. "Well, there's no time to kill the messenger!" She chuckled at her joke. "I've a busy morning. Ten minutes to get uptown for a massage, little touch-up on my hair, eyebrows, nails, the whole thing. I'm celebrating!" She beamed, "Did I tell you? It's our thirtieth!"

She must have seen me wince because she said, "Trust me sweetie, you'll get over this. There are a thousand men out there who must be dying to meet you."

She patted her hair. It did need a touch-up.

"Oops! Time's up. Really must run. You take care! We'll get together soon. Have coffee. But for now, I just wanted you to know that you are in everybody's thoughts. Bye-bye!"

She slipped out the door. Her steps echoed as she walked down the hallway. A hollow dead sound.

I felt as if I had been sliced in half.

I acted on automatic. I cleaned. I polished every piece of everything. Her words played over and over again. When there was nothing left to dust, or polish, or arrange, I made a phone call. I needed to talk to someone. I called Vincent.

Vincent owned Getchell Hill Boots below my shop on the first floor at Pier 70. Vincent had become my skiing buddy. I was one of the many women he found amusing, available, and acceptable. He had a quirky sense of humor and I adored him because he'd say things like, "How could that idiot husband of yours have left such a good skier?" or "I'll add you to my

harem. Number twenty-six. An honored position."
Vincent could make me laugh and he could make me forget I was waiting for a marriage to mend.

The phone rang.

"Getchell Hill Boots."

"Vincent."

"Yes, my chick-a-dee. What's up?"

I could barely speak. He must have noticed the pause, because he asked, "Are you okay?"

"No, I'm not okay."

"Robbed? Beaten? Is the wild-foot massager back? (Reference to a crazy who had entered my shop the month before, complimented me on my clogs, asked to see how the shoe was constructed—naïve as a toad, I handed him my clog—and then he knelt and began to massage my foot, which creeped me out, as well it should have, for later in that week he was arrested in downtown Seattle for grabbing a shoe after pushing a woman to the sidewalk. Vincent, of course, had found the story amusing.)

"No. Worse. Much worse."

"Well, don't keep me in suspense. Blurt it out!"

"She's pregnant."

"Who is the fecund *she*?"

"His girlfriend. She's pregnant." It was as if the words had been wrenched from under my right rib. The words sounded hollow, strange, unreal, weird, peculiar, wrong. I waited for Vincent to say something.

"Vincent, are you there?"

"I'm thinking. I'm thinking."

"Thinking what?" I wanted to shout at him, "Don't think! Say this is tragic! Life is unbearable! Horrible! Unfair! Devastating!"

I waited.

Then Vincent said exactly what I never would have expected, but exactly what I needed to hear.

He said, "Does that make you an *auntie*?"

I burst into laughter. His response was so insane. So right.

I hung up the phone, reached for the phone book, and called Phyllis Johnson, the meanest, toughest divorce attorney in town.

CHAPTER FOUR
MOVING ON

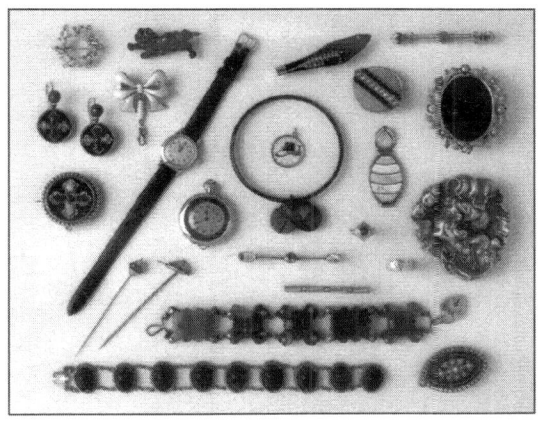

A selection of Antique jewelry

The divorce attorney, under the demands of a busy schedule, suggested I work with one of her associates, Wolfgang Anderson. At that time, Wolf was not the noted divorce attorney he is today. He was new to law, intent upon proving himself, and he made the process of obtaining a divorce nearly painless. Wolf told me, "As much as you can decide between you and your soon-to-be, be-glad-he's-gone husband, the less it will cost." With that exhortation, he nailed what soon became a single motivating factor: financial survival.

My soon-to-be ex and I met once, over dinner at Boondocks, Sundecker, and Greenthumbs. Seated behind a large fern where my tears were less observable by other patrons, we agreed on the division of property. I got the house. He got the art collection and a promise that I would pay him ten thousand dollars in one year. Wolf charged me $150.

In the end, I sold the house. The money from the sale sustained me through the years my business was not profitable.

Single, I faced major changes. The biggest change happened almost immediately. The change was based on lack of muscle. I had no manpower to help move large, heavy items.

For instance: a Monarch stove with double warming ovens, an extra large fire box and a hot water reservoir weighs about five hundred pounds. The stove breaks down into top plates, chrome skirts, splayed feet and, of course, the firebox, the warming ovens, and the water reservoir—all an elaborate three-dimensional jigsaw puzzle. It took me two hours to move the Monarch stove, piece by piece, from my van into the front shop window. It took another hour to reassemble the stove. Once in the window, the stove was magnificent. I stood back to admire its freshly blackened and freshly plated chrome glory. Like a doting mother, I removed the last of the fingerprints from the gleaming chrome. As I stood admiring my work, a customer walked in and inquired, "What are you asking for the stove?"

"Eight hundred dollars."

"You've got a sale!"

I wanted to yell, "No, you can't have it! I just trucked this stove three hundred miles. It has been on display five minutes." Instead I wrote the receipt and with a forced smile said, "Yes, of course, I'll gladly deliver."

I needed to find something to sell that weighed less. Way less.

And this is how that happened: Vi Kelly Barker, the doyenne of the antique world on the West Coast, offered a private class to five antique dealers. We gathered around her exquisite Queen Anne table where she placed a selection of silver flatware or porcelain figurines or Victorian jewelry or Fabergé Russian enamels or French lacquered boxes. She passed around each piece. We touched each piece. We examined each piece. For instance, a Meissen figurine of a shepherd boy was introduced with Vi's explanation. She drew our attention to the glaze, the delicate painting, the fineness, the marks, the age, the rarity, and then told us the value. We gently passed the figurine from one person to the next. The lesson ended when we had no more questions and she had told us all she knew. Under Vi's tutelage, she transformed each object—the same object which minutes before I would have dismissed as an expensive tchotchka.

At Vi's Wednesday class, following the Tuesday I delivered the Monarch stove, our lesson focused on jewelry. She placed before us a tray holding a Victorian enamel pendant, a gold Etruscan-style bracelet, a swag necklace, and four platinum, filigree, diamond rings. The jewelry was elegant, singular, beautiful. I held the amethyst swag necklace up to my neck. It was nearly weightless! It was eight hundred dollars! There was no soot, no need to clean, no replating.

I purchased the piece. Back at the shop I draped the necklace over a velvet form. A week later it sold. I gift-wrapped it. I placed it in a store sack. I handed it to the customer. Like Peter on the road to Damascus, this swag necklace resulted in a total redirection of my business.

After I would sell a piece of china, a cut glass bowl, or a silver fish slice, I would drive south to Vi's and replace the sold item with a piece of jewelry from her selection. Her dealer discount was generous. She allowed me to lay-away items. She shared her knowledge. She let me borrow books from her library.

"How nice to see you again," she said one morning. "Tell me exactly what you are doing."

I told her about the Monarch. I told her I was replacing each antique item in the store with a piece of jewelry.

"Let's have a cup of tea and talk."

It was then Vi gave me one of the best lessons ever. She said, "You can't afford to buy everything from me. Do this. Go to Globe Antiques. Go to Chelsea Antiques. Attend the big shows in Portland, Olympia, and Seattle. Make a pilgrimage to the Hillsborough Show in California. Find the best. Where you find the best, you will soon make discoveries. For instance," she held up a thimble-sized drinking glass, "See this? I went to the Dick Matilla show. This was for sale in one of the best booths in the show. They had no idea what it was. I bought it for twenty dollars. I knew something they didn't know. This glass is an early-American shot glass. The glass is worth one hundred dollars. That's what you need to do. You need to learn more than your competition. Focus on jewelry and pretty soon you will know more than everyone else, and I guarantee you, you will find the buys."

I followed Vi's advice. Slowly I began to accumulate a substantial selection of antique jewelry. I studied each piece. More knowledge led to excitement. More excitement led to more sales. More sales led to the next find. In the process, I fell in love with antique jewelry.

The difficult moment came when I made my last trip to Spokane. I had to tell my parents I no longer needed the collectables and the furniture they'd been providing. Mom was the most upset. Dad, it appeared, was ready for the change. I think he had worn himself out stripping furniture, repairing drawers, replacing pulls, rebuilding whatever needed restoration. After I broke the news, Dad excused himself and went into the front room and turned on the television. I could hear the sports announcer calling the plays. At least he had time now to get back to his favorite sports programs.

Mom reached for my hand and made a last attempt to thwart the change. She looked me in the eye and challenged me with the words: "You don't know anything about jewelry!"

"Right. But I didn't know anything about the antique business when I started five years ago." It was a tough discussion. I felt like a traitor.

I shared with Mom the problems I was facing as a single woman, the difficulty of moving furniture, driving to Spokane by myself. I explained my desire to focus on one part of the antique world. Knowing everything about everything in the world of antiques seemed overwhelming. I could not imagine becoming a generalist like Vi Kelly, who seemed to know everything about anything antique. I needed to specialize. Mom's next sentence cut through my thoughts.

"But does anyone buy it?" Mom asked.

"Buy what?"

"Antique jewelry?"

I winced. Mom always had the right questions.

"Well, once in awhile. I need to get an identity as an antique jewelry authority."

"An authority? I know you beat every kid in the block at marbles. You learned to throw a baseball better than your brothers. But an authority? Don't you need a degree or something?"

"If there was a degree to get, I'd go get it. There are classes, but I'd have to move to London or New York to take them. For now, I'm doing exactly what I did when I taught at The Laboratory School. I'm learning by doing. For instance, look at my ring." I showed her the diamond ring I had purchased from Vi. "It's filigree platinum from the 1920s. The stone weighs fifty points or half-a-carat. It is G color. SI1 clarity." I stopped to remember every detail Vi had taught me about the ring. "It's fabricated, not cast."

"Well, that's something!" Mom said, beaming her motherly, haven't-I-a-smart-daughter smile. But the smile faded. I could see she felt rejected. Without saying so, I knew she would miss my treks to Spokane. The business had wrapped our lives together and given Mom and Dad a focus—a focus they loved sharing, both with me and with each other.

"Well, if anyone can do it, you can!" She gave my

fingers a squeeze and stood. "Time for dinner." She reached for the hot pads, opened the oven and removed the aluminum roaster. The fragrant smell of roast beef filled the kitchen. As she sliced the crisp brown meat, she asked, "What did it cost?"

"Two thousand four hundred dollars."

Mom's shoulders pulled back as if she had been hit with an electric jolt. Carving knife in hand, she waved it at me as if to erase the exorbitant amount of money. "Don't ever tell your father! He won't understand. That's pricier than anything he's spent hours and hours refinishing." With those words, the discussion ended. Dad came into the kitchen at the quarter break to see how we were doing and suggested we load a few items in the truck.

And that's how the transition continued. Slowly I sold off the items Mom and Dad had waiting in the garage. It took two more trips. The storytelling of finds and treasures diminished. Trips to Spokane dwindled to Christmas and birthday celebrations. I never quite got over feeling that I let my parents down.

Back at work in Seattle, the biggest challenge I faced was finding customers to buy antique jewelry.

I created a flyer:
LEARN THE HISTORY OF YOUR JEWELRY! JOIN IN THE DISCOVERY OF UNFOUND TREASURES! LEARN WHAT IS GOOD, BETTER, BEST!

And so began the classes I taught. Each class was limited to six people (exactly the number I could fit around the jewelry cases). I promised to share all the mistakes I had ever made. The class lasted six weeks. Two-hour sessions. Thirty-five dollars per person. I studied furiously each week to prepare the next lesson. Vi loaned me books from her library. Whatever the public library had to offer, I studied. I made worksheets. I reproduced diagrams of stones. I took slides. I slowly began to accumulate knowledge about antique jewelry. Each week's lesson took shape. What I learned, I taught.

Class members brought their own jewelry. They were encouraged to bring photographs of their ancestors wearing the jewelry. They brought stories surrounding the jewelry. Their stories helped date the jewelry. The dated pieces became touchstones. I took photographs of their pieces and began a notebook for future reference.

Together we learned to decipher hallmarks (information Vi had taught in her dealer class when we studied British silver). I bought the Dorothy T. Rainwater book, *American Jewelry*. My knowledge of marks grew. My library grew. Often my knowledge was only pages ahead of my students.

Class members spread the word to their friends. Every other month I had six new people taking the class. Within the year, speaking engagements came my way. In the next five years I spoke at collector's clubs, women's teas, the Washington Athletic Club. These lectures were demanding. I needed more slides. I found more books. Every lecture took an average of fifty hours of research. Over the years the slide library grew into hundreds of slides. On occasion I was invited to speak to national groups focused on antique jewelry.

"Who will buy antique jewelry?" my mother had asked. Just as I had purchased from Vi, my students purchased from me. The business grew. My knowledge grew.

But my knowledge didn't include smarts about being single. I learned how to manage a business while I was being stalked.

CHAPTER FIVE
SURVIVING A STALKER

"Hi! How ya doin?" a six-foot-two-inch, auburn-haired, muscular man walked into Vanity Fair, all cheer and good greeting. It never crossed my mind he was a stalker.

In the next nine months I learned that evil hides. Evil does not come with horns and a tail. Evil does not chuckle under its breath. Evil does not wear a blowing red cape. Evil comes with a smile and a jaunty "hello." Evil comes when you are vulnerable, silly, and stupid, and in this case, single.

Bruce and I divorced in 1975, after thirteen years. Being single subtly worked a transformation in me. I, who thought of myself as invincible, wasn't. I was vulnerable. With the break-up of the marriage, I yearned for reassurance that I was attractive and interesting, desirable and sexy. That assurance came in the person of the cheerful six-footer. For my own safety, even now, thirty years later, I'll refer to him as L. M., (not his real initials). I didn't know then, what I know now—evil can enter your life with the words, "Hi, how ya doin?" Cheery.

Nothing about L.M. appeared evil. In fact, he was down-right attractive. L.M. was well-coiffed, casually dressed, neither too ostentatious nor too casual. He was just right. He walked over to the first case in my shop and studied a set of porcelain figurines: a shepherd and a shepherdess. "Do they have the cross-swords mark?" he asked. If you want to impress an antique dealer, that is one way to do it: be a muscular man, in well-fitting jeans, and ask about the mark on Meissen porcelain.

Immediately I was by his side, unlocking the case to show him the blue over-glazed mark. Our fingers touched.

"And a great price!" he said. He was positive, energetic, and knowledgeable. "I'd be sorely tempted to purchase this set of figures, but I have a twelve inch set, almost identical."

And he was a collector.

There were no computers then. And even if there were, I'm not sure I would have done a background check on this man. He was so charming. So unassuming. Even gracious. At that time, I was naïve enough to think that if someone was dangerous, or mean, or inappropriate, I'd certainly know. Sure, I had heard of a friend of a friend, paranoid and obsessed, who hired a private detective to be sure her newly acquired boyfriend wasn't after her money. He wasn't. She spent two thousand dollars for nothing. She married the guy and they had just celebrated their fifth anniversary. Besides, this was Seattle. The friend of a friend lived in Los Angeles where one had to be more careful.

It would be another two years before I read the front page story in *The Seattle Times* about a recent immigrant from Sweden. She was a woman in her mid-twenties. She rode the bus everyday to her job at Bell Telephone. She sat directly behind the bus driver on her way to and from Capitol Hill. Two witnesses at her murder trial testified that the woman sat up front and close to the driver because it appeared he gave her a feeling of safety. The two witnesses testified that in their estimation the driver paid her an inordinate amount of attention. They were concerned for her but it never dawned on them to warn her about him or even to caution her. The bus driver seemed like an ordinary guy. Maybe a little lonesome. He murdered her. Who would have guessed such a mild-mannered man was evil? The witnesses used the word "evil."

L.M. visited the shop again, later that week. He asked questions and made knowledgeable comments: "Is this Art Nouveau style or Jungenstil? Nice example of hand engraving. I haven't seen a slice server like this in years. Did you know that the knife in a fish-set was called a slice? I just learned that recently."

I was impressed. The way he handled objects was impressive. His questions were impressive. Who wouldn't have been taken with his style, his manners, his knowledge?

He took my card as he left and said, "Lovely place! My name's L.M. I'll be back!"

Five minutes later the phone rang. "This is L.M. I couldn't wait. I know this is a bit abrupt, but I'm downstairs at the Smuggler Restaurant and I was wondering if I waited, you might consider joining me for a light dinner?"

The invitation was easy to accept. What more would a single woman want? A new interest. Someone attentive. A "light" dinner. Just the use of the word "light" gave the invitation a breezy, innocent air.

After two months of dating, L.M. was even more attractive. He was verbally quick. He had a deep and diverse knowledge of antiques—porcelain to silver to oriental rugs. He embraced new experiences, which led to a theatre trip to see Midsummer Night's Dream. He quoted Shakespeare back to me over late night drinks. He took me to soccer games and then deep-sea fishing. His energy was contagious and compelling. His energy attracted and held me. Only one thing I didn't notice: his energy hid aggressive, out-of-control anger.

He yelled at slow drivers and he yelled at people crossing the crosswalk. He yelled at the microwave when he pushed the wrong buttons. He yelled at my dog. Then he yelled at me.

The outbursts were always momentary and if I grew silent or if he made me cry, he apologized deeply and he apologized with flowers or notes or poems. He could not have been more sincere.

His anger came and went like quick-silver. As time passed, his outbursts escalated. His words cut: "If you're such a smart, college graduate, why didn't you…" and he would sneer and find fault. The list of things I didn't do right grew.

Then one day I had had enough. He yelled at me for not waiting for him to open the car door. I yelled back. My response scared me. I came from a family where no one yelled. I told him I'd had enough. I told him he had to leave. To never call me again. I stormed down the path to my house. For once he didn't come begging for forgiveness. His tires squealed as he left.

Two days later he showed up as I was closing the shop. He had a dozen red roses. He looked crushed. He missed me horribly. He hadn't meant to get angry. He hadn't meant to yell over such a stupid thing. He begged for another chance.

I succumbed. For a few days he was the sunny man who had walked into my shop that first day.

Then the verbal slam came when I didn't fill the gas tank to the top. He yelled at me in front of the gas station attendant. I rode in silence. I silently practiced what I would say.

We drove down into my driveway. I opened the door and before he could get out, I snapped, "It's over. We're finished."

He didn't try to win me back. He yelled at me to get away from his fucking car. I didn't deserve anyone. Ever. No wonder my husband left. I was a worthless piece of shit.

Three days later he called as if nothing had happened. Over the phone I told him there were no more chances. I would not see him again. I told him there was nothing he could say or do.

"What about my stuff?" he demanded. "You've got my best cooking pot, my complete Shakespeare, my Roethke book!"

I told him my parents were coming the next day for a visit. I told him I'd put everything of his in a box. It would be on the front porch. He could pick it up the next day while I was at work.

When I came home the box was gone and my parents had arrived.

I told my parents everything about L.M. Mom and Dad stayed for an extra two days. L.M. didn't call. Hopefully he was gone forever. The time came for my parents to drive home to Spokane. Mom and Dad gave me extra long hugs. I assured them I would be okay. How I hated to see them leave.

That night the hang-up phone calls began.

I'd answer the phone. Silence. On the fifth call I yelled in the phone that I knew it was him. He chuckled and hung up.

The next day I called the police. The operator connected me to the Domestic Violence Division. They told me I needed to make a police report. They would send someone out. Two officers showed up in a patrol car. They assured me that over time, domestic problems such as this usually disappeared. But in the meantime, I might want to install new locks. Add double locks while

I was at it. Oh, and I should change my phone number. I was to call if there were more problems.

I walked up the path to where their patrol car was parked. Before they drove away, the officer rolled down the window and said, "Given how isolated your house is, you might consider a restraining order." And as an after thought he said, "You might consider moving."

"How do I do that? Get a restraining order?" I asked.

"Look under bondsmen in the yellow pages. There are a slew of them. It'll cost you fifty bucks."

He held out his card and said, "If things get worse, call."

They drove away. I looked at the card. His name was Marshall Longtin. I would have laughed if I hadn't been so scared.

That night there were twenty phone calls. The next day I got an unlisted phone number and went to a bondsman on First Avenue. At the bondsman's office I paid fifty dollars to have the paper work done. The man told me it would be another fifty dollars to have the papers served.

"What if I wait and don't serve the papers? Maybe he won't come back. Maybe I don't need to serve them."

"Lady, you can do whatever you want. You just need to tell us when."

That night there were no phone calls. Perhaps L.M. had given up. Had disappeared. I decided to wait. Besides, what if they served the papers and it embarrassed him in front of his family or his friends and it made him even angrier? Two nights there were no phone calls.

And then…

L.M. called the shop. He didn't say hello. He said, "How's Loehler?"

Something in his voice made me know things were worse. I screamed into the phone, "What have you done with my dog?"

"Why would I do anything with your dog?" I could almost hear the sneer in his voice. The way he asked, told me. He had done something with my Husky, Loehler. I lost complete control. I screamed into the phone, "You son-of-a-bitch." I could barely hold back the tears.

"I'm not going to talk to you when you're out of control. Your dog is as worthless as you." He hung up the phone.

I called the bondsman and put the second fifty-dollar charge on my Visa. It was time to serve the restraining order. I never saw Loehler again.

For the next month I lived in fear. I changed my phone number six times. Each time I was guaranteed the number was unlisted. A day would pass and then around two o'clock in the morning, the phone would ring. It would ring over and over and over again. When I answered there would be silence. I would yell at him to leave me alone. I'd hang up. The phone would ring again. And again. Thirty times. Forty times.

I demanded to talk to someone at the phone company who could help me. I got the Vice President of Community Affairs. He asked, "Are you sure you're not giving him your phone number?" I knew he didn't believe me when I said I hadn't even seen this person in three weeks.

Then my friend Vincent began receiving hang-up phone calls. (Over the next six months, whoever I dated, received hang-up phone calls. I learned much later that L.M. copied the license plate of my dates and then he called the Bureau of Licenses in Olympia. He was able to obtain the phone number of the owner of the car. It took ten more years before there was a law that prohibited giving out phone numbers related to a car license.)

When the calls continued, I called Marshall Longtin. He was out to my house within the hour.

"Keep a detailed report of every phone call." He hesitated, and then he said, "I hate to tell you this; there is nothing we can do until he does something. Phone calls don't count."

"He does *something*? Like what?"

"Does something physical."

He wasn't saying it, but the warning was clear.

The next time I saw Marshall Longtin I told him what I had decided to do.

"I'm going to buy a gun," I told him.

"Don't buy a gun. People get shot with their own guns. Do this: Nothing. Don't give him any satisfaction. Hang up immediately when he calls. No matter what he does, make no response. You respond? He gets what he wants."

Officer Longtin guaranteed me that in ninety-nine percent of domestic violence cases, no response makes a stalker find someone else. I would never need to use the gun.

I didn't ask about the one percent. I didn't question his use of the word, "stalker."

That night, there were thirty-seven phone calls between two and four o'clock. At nine o'clock the next morning I drove south past Vi's to a shop I had passed dozens of times going to class.

I parked in front of Big Jim's Pawn and Gun Shop.

"Can we help you, Missy?" said an older man in a plaid flannel shirt and coveralls. He laconically turned in his office chair, looked over the top of his newspaper, and nodded as if he knew I needed time to walk up and down the ten-foot case of hand guns.

Dozens of guns were on display. It made me angry to think I had to spend any money on L.M. Besides, I wasn't even the kind of person who would ever buy a gun. I was for gun control. I wrote letters to my congressman. Today, I stopped when I got to the display with $39.95 Specials.

"I need a gun," I said.

"What for?" he asked, rocking forward and lumbering to his feet to join me at the counter.

"To protect myself," I said.

"How about I interest you in a can of mace?"

"No, I need a gun."

It appeared from his slow movements, his

quizzical glance, that he thought I had made the wrong choice. I told him mace wouldn't do it.

I left with the $39.95 Special.

A week later Officer Longtin came by to see how I was doing.

I told him that the phone calls had not stopped. I told him I still hadn't found my dog. I told him an empty liquor bottle had been left in my mail box. I told him that blossoms of the rhododendron had been chopped off. Then I told him I had purchased a gun.

"I told you not to buy a gun."

"I couldn't figure out any way to be safe."

"Where is it?"

"It's under my mattress."

"Oh, great. Just where you can get it. Please go get the gun."

I did. I proudly told him I had already been to the shooting range to practice.

"How did you do?"

"I didn't do very well. In fact I couldn't hit the target."

"I'm not surprised," he said as he examined the short, stubby gun.

The plastic on the handle looked like raspberry-swirl ice cream.

"Listen to me and listen carefully. See the barrel of this gun? See how short it is? If you're going to use this gun, be sure of one thing."

He waited for me to ask.

"What's that?"

He sighed, moved the tiny gun from one hand to anther. He said, "When you shoot, be sure he's on top of you."

I called Vincent to let him know what Officer Longtin had said. I knew he would laugh. But that night, a strange thing happened. There were no phone calls. It was as if L.M. knew about the gun. I was paranoid enough to think that somehow he was able to listen in on my phone calls. If he knew enough to get six unlisted numbers, he knew enough to cut into my phone line. The next morning I called the phone company. A vice president at the phone company assured me what I feared wasn't possible. I had the distinct impression the executive was keeping a log on me like I was keeping a log on L.M. I believed he thought I was crazy.

That's most of the story.

I was one of the lucky survivors of stalking, but I never got over the fear or the caution. For years, if there was a hang-up phone call at the shop or at home I would write down the day and the time. I never knew if it was L.M.

Six months after the last phone call, L.M. came into my shop. I dialed 911. As he stood staring at me, I demanded he leave. He was gone by the time the police arrived. I made another police report.

He sent postcards when he traveled.

One day he called begging me not to hang up. He

told me he had just lost his son. I hung up.

I never spoke to him again. The stalking ended.

Thirty years later I read about the memorial service for Rebecca Griego, 26. Rebecca was shot by her ex-boyfriend-turned stalker. She was a program coordinator at the Runstad Center in the University of Washington's Gould Hall. After the stalker shot her, after he was sure she was dead, he shot himself.

I know one thing for certain. L.M. was capable of shooting me.

He would never have shot himself.

What is disturbing about the Rebecca Griego story is that she had told people. She had notified the police. It appears nothing much has changed.

I learned a horrible truth from the experience of being stalked. I was not alone. According to the U.S. National Center for Victims of Crime, over one million women a year are stalked: Seventy-seven percent of the victims know their stalker: Fifty-nine percent of the victims are stalked by an intimate partner: Eighty-one percent of the women are stalked by a former intimate partner and eventually are physically assaulted by that partner: Seventy-three percent of intimate partner stalkers verbally threaten victims with physical violence: The average duration of stalking is 1.8 years: Twenty-eight percent of the female victims who went to the trouble to secure a protective order found the order useless.

The stalkers pay no mind. The stalkers continue stalking.

I can still hear Marshall Longtin say, "There's nothing we can do until he does something to you." I wonder if Rebecca Griego was told the same thing.

CHAPTER SIX
WHEN THE RIGHT ONE

Greek dancing at our wedding

"When you put the fork in the potato you know when it's done."

This brilliant sentence was Mom's response and her blessing when I announced I planned, after three years of single-hood, after swearing I'd never, ever again wear a wedding ring, after giving up on men entirely, to marry again. I'd known Don for exactly five weeks. To this day I believe that potato sentence to be brilliant and perceptive.

Five weeks before this phone call, I had given up on men entirely. In place of any man in my life, I was now running five miles in the morning and at night.

Building A Business, Building A Life

I had also enrolled in a painting class at the University of Washington. I had joined a Great Books group. I had reordered a single season ticket to Act Theatre. And what turned out to be a most fateful decision, I began classes in Greek dancing.

September 12, 1978, I waited at the Greek Village for one of my employees. She belonged to a local exhibition dancing group, Radost. She knew I had been taking Greek dancing lessons. She suggested we meet at the Greek Village after work one evening. I went directly from work. My employee was late.

The restaurant hostess ushered me to one of the small circular tables that surrounded the dance floor. I watched the small stage where the musicians tuned. Seconds later the strum and pop of the balalaika, oud, and bouzouki bounced from the speakers and the dance floor filled. Once assembled, the circle of dancers slowly began to move to the sweet Syrto. I joined the circle and fell into the easy, melodic rhythm of the simple steps. Hands extended, the circle undulated around the room. It was almost like dancing alone, nothing to think about except the lift of the foot to the sweet swell of the music.

Except, I did notice this fine fellow on the other side of the circle. He danced with an easy grace. He spoke to the woman on his right. She smiled. He spoke to the woman on his left. She laughed. He was at home in the dance and on the dance floor. He moved with a gentle ease, each step defined and perfect. I didn't stare, but I certainly noticed.

When the musicians took a break, I watched that gentleman from across the room. Interesting. He'd sit

Building A Business, Building A Life

at a table of one to three women. He'd chat for awhile. Then he would proceed to the next table.

The music resumed. The Greek men were there to prove their glorious Greekness. To show the lineage of all the years they had watched their fathers and their grandfathers, they brilliantly danced the Syrtaki. The dance allowed the Greeks to show off their masculinity, their agility, their virility.

The button-downed guy, who had caught my eye, was noticeable for a number of reasons:

> - His suntan and plaid shirt with leather elbows
> - His rather apparent English-German-Norwegian demeanor
> - His proficient style as he danced—compact, precise, controlled, as if a structural engineer had brought all of his skills to the flamboyant world of Greek dancing.

It crossed my mind that perhaps this man was part-owner of the restaurant. Why would anyone so methodically work the room?

I watched as each dance ended. This man escorted both the woman on his left and the woman on his right back to their table. With a slight bow, he said his thanks, turned and introduced himself to the women at the next table. He seemed to know everyone, or if he didn't he made a point of meeting everyone.

About nine o'clock, my employee called the restaurant and the waitress came to tell me she wouldn't be joining me, she had a flat tire and had taken the bus home.

On the dance floor, the steps became more demanding. Two circles formed. The inner circle filled with dancers who knew each step, each repetition. The outside circle consisted of beginners or intermediate dancers, who stood behind one of the accomplished dancers, and mimicked the steps until they were ready to join the inner circle. A lively Syrtaki brought everyone to the floor. You could see each person imagined Zorba as a partner—hands held high, dreamy, as if the music itself had said, "Teach me to dance."

Feet moved, cut, swung, tapped, and slid, and the dancers pushed the circle into a jiggidy caterpillar of action. As the intensity of the music increased, the Greek men took over the floor. And the mystery man? Never missed a step. He danced until only five or six men remained, each dancer taking his turn in a series of intricate slaps and stamps and steps.

At the beginning of the next dance, I made a point of moving onto the dance floor so that I stood next to this mystery man. The Hasapiko was a breeze compared to the Syrtaki. I loved dancing next to someone who knew the steps, understood the hesitations, swayed in perfect rhythm, and captured the subtleties of each step. We didn't speak, but at the end of the dance he led me back to my table, smiled, said, "thank you" and returned to visiting with the occupants of the last table he had visited on his journey.

Orderly, to say the least. Four more tables and it would be my turn.

When he was one table away, the musicians announced that the next dance would be a Karsilamis. I stayed in the outer circle, dancing directly behind "The man." After the tenth repetition, I had the steps. Then magic! The man turned, let loose the hand to his right, and invited me into the inner circle. And when the dance ended? He walked me back to my table, but immediately returned to his last visited table.

I was next. It crossed my mind that maybe he was selling insurance. What a dreadful thought. And then?

"Hi, I'm Don Bell."

"Hi, I'm Karen"

"How long have you been with the group?"

"I've never been here before. First time."

"Did you just join?"

"Join? I didn't think you had to join anything. I was supposed to meet one of my employees here, but she had a car problem. She dances with Radost." (Notice, I said "she" so he'd not think I had a date with a guy who would enter at any moment.)

"I'm talking to everyone in the group."

"You're what?"

"It's why I'm sitting here at your table."

I must have looked totally confused. I was totally confused.

"I have strict instructions from Dorothy."

"Who's Dorothy?"

"Your dance instructor." Slowly I could see it begin to dawn on this nice fellow that he had made a wrong assumption. "You're not part of the group, are you?"

"What group?"

"The Divorce Support Group!" He began to

laugh. "I'm supposed to be sure everyone in Dorothy's Divorce Support Group is greeted and made to feel welcome. My instructions."

It was a good story. It was a great story.

And? He walked me to my car. The next day he called. We had dinner.

Five weeks later we decided to get married.

It's been over thirty years. A fabulous thirty-plus years.

CHAPTER SEVEN
THINKING BIG, THEN BIGGER

In front of the Facèrè Salon

What is the strategy for maintaining a business while getting divorced, while being stalked, while falling in love? I did the most illogical thing. I enrolled in the University of Washington to get another degree. In painting. Why? Blame Joan Baez. She sang a song in the sixties about how the least admirable entity, right up there with the military-industrial complex, was business. The perennial cocktail party question, as we all know, is "And what do you do?" Because it embarrassed me to say I ran a business, I went back to school so that I could answer, "I'm a painter."

The university allowed me to enroll in a single

Building A Business, Building A Life

class each quarter. I'd take a three-hour studio class in the morning and arrive at work with cerulean blue under my fingernails. It took eleven years to get that Bachelor of Fine Arts. They were eleven great years. No matter the ups and downs of business, while I painted, there were no worries—it was me, the canvas, the paint, the brushes, the turpentine, the idea.

Juggling painting, a new marriage, and a growing business made me aware that I needed advice. I needed someone who knew more about business than I did. I needed fresh eyes. I needed a clearer vision. I needed someone with extensive business experience. I had lasted three years and had increased sales, but I also had increased expenses.

For instance, I had attended an auction in Monroe, Washington. I remember thinking, "The more I bid, the more money I'll make!" (A totally irrational thought, but I do recall being overwhelmed with that exact idea.) The tenth item at the auction was a tray of eight jewelry items. The bid quickly grew from thirty dollars to one hundred and twenty dollars. I won! But, of course, once the excitement and fun of the auction disappeared, I realized I had bid more than the items were worth.

I needed help. I found exactly what I needed in the *Puget Sound Business Journal*. An article, "Choosing a Business Consultant," led me to Stephen Fletcher. I called. We talked. We met. I hired him. It was a wise business move.

Stephen Fletcher, who later transformed Stewart Brothers Coffee into Seattle's Best Coffee and made Jim Stewart a multimillionaire (I'm proud to say I introduced them), was exactly what I was looking for. Stephen loves numbers, ratios, percentages, spreadsheets, financial statements, and has all of the other hard-nosed, left-brained qualities required to run a business. He is analytical, logical, rational, objective, and thorough. He moves thoughtfully and makes considered decisions. As we worked together I learned to respect his ideas, and more important, I learned to act on them.

For instance, Stephen suggested the business have a newsletter. The next week I had a mock-up. One month later we published the first newsletter. A year later we hired a professional team headed by Tom Peterson and the newsletter became a staple of the business.

Stephen stated it was time the business had a full-time employee. I put an ad in the *Times*. We received twenty responses and of those twenty we interviewed six. Don, Stephen, and I interviewed each candidate. Twice. The first interview was very formal. We three sat behind a table, asked written questions, and gave a numerical score to each candidate.

The second interview we served coffee and croissants, play-acted a sale, and learned how a candidate acted in an easy-going situation. What an interesting exercise! One young woman had scored high in the first interview, but in the second, when she relaxed, her use of the English language vanished and by the third time she responded, "Cool," we were ready for the next candidate.

Two interviewees outshone everyone: Lael Hagan and Jim Morgan. Lael, with a double degree in art and history, could write and speak clearly, loved jewelry, and was ready to begin immediately. Jim was a music teacher recently riffed from the Seattle Public Schools. He was charming, pleasant, passed the play-acting sale situation with ease, and had a great sense of humor. It didn't hurt when at the end of the interview Jim looked directly at me and said, "I truly want this job." How could I not want to hire him!

Stephen led me to believe that with the energy of these two candidates, with their skill, their smarts, their enthusiasm, their demeanor, they would create enough business to pay for both of their salaries. I hired both.

For the next three years we were an unbeatable team. Then Lael won a scholarship to study in New York at the Gemological Institute of America and Jim was hired to teach music in Nuremburg, Germany. Over the past forty years I've had the most remarkable employees. Lael and Jim were two of the very best.

One idea of Stephen's scared me to death—a board of advisors. Within these parameters:

- They would be volunteers
- They would be professionals in their own right
- They would meet quarterly, for exactly two hours
- They would have access to all of my books and ideas
- I would serve cookies

I can remember thinking, who would give up precious time to serve on a board of advisors for cookies?

Stephen's answer:

- Everyone wishes they owned a small business

- They will be interesting people
- They will enjoy getting to know each other
- They will be flattered that you carefully consider their ideas

Invitations were extended to Vi Kelly (antiques dealer extraordinaire), Sandy McAusland (inventor, engineer), Nancy Davidson-Short (editor of Sunset Magazine), Don Bell (architect, husband), and Howard Breskin (attorney). I invited and they agreed.

The day of the first advisory board meeting I was excited, anxious, apprehensive, and concerned. Stephen assured me the evening was not only going to be interesting and helpful, but, without a doubt, everyone would have a good time. To control my fears, I brewed coffee, laid out a platter of cookies, dusted the cases for the third time, and tried not to watch the clock—all the time convinced no one would show.

They did show. As each person arrived, the room grew more comfortable with chatter and at exactly 7:15 I asked everyone to fill their coffee cups and be seated. We sat around the three spokes of the jewelry cases that occupied the center of the room. Each person introduced him or herself and, as Stephen suggested, told why he or she had agreed to participate. Vi Kelly, the antique dealer, boldly said, "I'm here because I'm twice Karen's age, I've twice the experience, and she needs me," and she raised a finger to make her final point, "No one should make the mistakes I made." Her words set the tone and the pace. We were ready to talk business.

Four times a year over the next two years we discussed every aspect of the business. I opened the books to their scrutiny. Sales. Returns Cost of goods. The board analyzed pricing, merchandise mix, salaries, employee benefits, cash flow, bank relationships, advertising, customer service—every possible part of the business.

The day came when we discussed whether or not it was time to move the business from the waterfront to a more up-scale location.

Vi suggested, "The islands."

I thought that wasn't a very good idea. Bainbridge? Vashon? Whidbey? All of the islands required riding a ferry and didn't seem populated enough to support an antique jewelry store.

"No! No! No!" Vi cut my objections short. "The Hawaiian Islands!"

What an amazing idea!

The next month Don and I flew to the Big Island with dreams of leisure living, sunny days, tourists with money to spend. We arrived to the smell of plumeria and headed to our hotel. We had high hopes, but we had no appointments and we had no letters of introduction. We visited a half-dozen leasing offices. We came away with brochures and kind smiles and the reality that rent on the island averaged $125 a square foot, about ten times the rent at Pier 70. All in all, the process was interesting, exciting, absorbing. But it was crazy. Once home, we realized we had just had a great vacation, but we truly did not want to have a business so far away from our roots. We gave up the idea of moving. Seattle was home, and home was where we wanted to stay.

However, the idea had been planted to find a new

location. I scoured Pioneer Square, First Avenue, Midtown, University Village, Bell Town, West Seattle.

I even met with the leasing agent of Bellevue Square, a shopping mall in the prosperous city of Bellevue. A twenty-minute drive from Seattle. The agent offered very attractive terms. I considered the lease for three days and then I called to decline. Astonished at my decline, Kemper Freeman, owner of the mall, called with an invitation to lunch.

"This is very strange," he said. "Rarely, if ever does anyone turn us down." He repeated all of the advantages of his mall. He truly wanted to know why I had made such a wrong choice. Facing his enthusiasm, I lost focus. I told him I would reconsider. But, as I drove across the floating bridge to beautiful Seattle, it was clear as clear could be. Seattle was the city I knew and the city I loved. I wasn't going to fly to Hawaii. I wasn't even going to drive across a bridge to Bellevue.

The proverbial door closing, door opening happened. In the center of the city, Sixth and Pike, I fell in love (falling in love is not the best way to choose a location), with the newly opened Sheraton Hotel.

It was obvious to me they needed a jewelry store. It never crossed my mind that they wouldn't give me a lease. It never crossed my mind that jewelry stores in hotels are usually considered over-priced and tasteless. It never crossed my mind that I couldn't afford the location. It certainly never crossed my mind that I might not make any money.

I called the Sheraton. I asked to speak to the manager. The secretary answered, "Sorry, Mr. Welly is on his way out of town. You'll have to call back."

I called the next week. Mustering a commanding voice, I asked for Mr. Welly. Not in.

I left a message.

Message never returned.

I continued to call. I'd call and he'd have a meeting, or would be going out of town, or would promise to call back. For over a month, he never called back.

I persisted.

On Wednesday, November 10, 1982 Mr. Welly caved. He agreed to meet at 11:00.

Stephen and I prepared a five-page business plan and placed it in a slick folder, and we made extra copies.

Mike Welly listened. He explained that he would have to speak to the owners. He made it clear that I needed $100,000 in merchandise. He made it clear that I would have to do all the tenant improvements. He also made it very clear that he doubted the viability of a store with only antique jewelry, as he didn't know anyone who wore antique jewelry. To the list of requirements he added that half the jewelry would have to be modern.

Roadblock, roadblock, roadblock ran through my mind.

I returned to Pier 70 and sent him a thank-you note and a twenty-dollar bottle of wine.

I waited two weeks and called again. This time he said I'd have to meet with two of the owners: Howard Wright and Jerry Anches. He gave me their numbers to arrange an appointment. I think he felt I'd never get through, it would take a couple more months, and maybe I would disappear.

Shuffle me off to Buffalo.

I called and strangely enough, I got a meeting with Jerry Anches and Howard Wright in two weeks. We would meet at Mike's office.

Jerry entered the room: slender, well-dressed, handsome in a kind of Al Pacino way, almost shy. Howard Wright followed him: round, hail-fellow-well-met-ish, boisterous, and friendly.

They had questions. They were up-front about the idea that I might not be the right person for their hotel. They were a large chain, didn't I know? What kind of experience did I have? What kind of money did I have?

Stephen and I were prepared. We had a three-year budget in place. We had brought ten of the most expensive pieces of jewelry from Vanity Fair. We had rehearsed any questions that we might be asked. We handed them a copy of our business plan:
- Cash flow for three years
- Business history
- Market evaluation
- Customer profile

We answered every question and showed them how we would meet all of their demands. At a certain point, Mike stood, leaned on his desk, knuckles supporting him, and said, "It's been a pleasure. We will be in touch with you." Meeting over. We hadn't a clue what they would say or do. We went down to the Sheraton café where I treated Stephen to lunch. I treated myself to a much-needed glass of wine.

By two o'clock I was back at Pier 70 and ordered

two large bouquets of roses. One for Jerry. One for Howard.

Negotiations continued for six months.

Like slow molasses, the lease was finally offered. Jerry Anches called to make an appointment. "Bring your pen!" It took less than five minutes. He shook my hand and then shared the story that the management boys had tried to stop the lease, but Jerry wanted me to know his word was his word and he'd told them, "No, she's good. It's a done deal." His parting words to me were, "Welcome aboard." At the door, just as I was leaving, Jerry said, recalling a conversation we had had during the negotiations, "Karen, I don't want to harp on the subject, but you should know you won't make it if you don't discount." I didn't argue "I'll think about it." What I didn't tell him was that I had learned enough about discounting, that merchants who discounted created a huge hole in their budgets and irritated customers more than pleased them. My advisory board confirmed my beliefs, along with what I experienced on a daily basis. We had spent an entire meeting discussing every nuance of discounting. Stephen had shared an article that showed the numbers. You lose when you discount. You lose believability. You lose stature. You lose money. There was no way I was going to discount.

Just recently, Jerry walked by the gallery at City Centre. He waved, and he called, "How's it going?" I answered, "I'm still here!" He smiled and gave me a thumbs up! I doubt he even remembered that discounting conversation.

CHAPTER EIGHT
GIVING A PARTY, GIVING A PARTY, GIVING A PARTY

A party at Century Square

Thanks to the Sheraton Hotel manager, Mike Welly, who agreed to that first meeting. Thanks to the owners, Jerry Anches and Howard Wright, who succumbed to my persistence. Thanks to the fact that I'd sold the property from my divorce just in time to meet the hotel's financial demands. Thanks to my architect husband who could design a perfect space. Thanks to my passion, my determination, my inability to think other than that I was the best tenant the Sheraton could possibly have—thanks to all of these things and the alignment of the stars, angels' blessings, luck and timing, Facèré Jewelry Salon opened on April

Building A Business, Building A Life

20, 1983. That was the first of three grand openings.

But before the doors opened, a check-off list of tasks had been accomplished:
- Name
- Logo, gift wrap, sacks, business card, and signage
- Invitations for the Grand Openings

First, the name. North Country Fair and Vanity Fair, the two shops at Pier 70, were great names for the rustic, waterfront setting. But we were moving uptown. Into a beautiful new hotel. Into a lobby that profiled Northwest artists. Next door to Fullers, Seattle's best restaurant. The new name had to fit the new location.

Choosing a name was a challenge. We were scheduled to meet with our attorney, Howard Breskin, to go over the hotel lease and to register our corporation. We needed a name to fit the space. We chose Facèré —an unpronounceable name.

We considered many choices: Karen's Shop, The Jewelry Store, Centuries, Treasures, First and Last, Choices. None of the names fit.

We wanted a sophisticated name. We wanted a singular name. We wanted a memorable name. We opened the dictionary.

Have you ever read a dictionary? The possibilities are endless. The choices are overwhelming.

And then? We found the right word: facient. The definition: present participle of *facere*, to make or to do, as in manufacture.

Perfecto! Facere.

But the word needed a little more. And because

Häagen-Dazs was a made-up word with a decorative umlaut, we decided we could do the same. But French. Accents, of course. Why not? We added two. Then, not to miss the international flavor of this single shop, we Italianated the pronunciation.

Roll the word off your tongue. Raise your eyebrows. Hold thumb to pointing finger as if you are twirling your very French mustache. Fah-cherry! So Facèré came into existence.

A wondrous name! To which we added the modifier, *Salon*.

Only one thing: we didn't think, even once, that Facèré would be difficult to pronounce. We didn't think, even once, that the word would be pronounced other than Fah-cherry. We were wrong. The name has been pronounced incorrectly in ways that would make you blush.

It is not unusual, even today, for the phone at the gallery to ring and when we answer, "Facèré Jewelry Art Gallery," silence follows. Then the caller hangs up. I'm convinced people are sitting around their kitchen table and someone says, "How do they say the name of that funny jewelry store?" An argument ensues. Then someone calls and we answer the phone. "Facèré." The debate ends. "It's not Fack-ery! It's Facèré! Like Gucci!"

Choosing a logo took weeks. First, we interviewed three design firms. We eventually chose John Hornall and Jack Anderson of Hornall/Anderson. We described the feeling of what we wanted to these two young designers and the image we wished our logo to convey:

Building A Business, Building A Life

sophistication, uniqueness, history, and the hand of the jeweler.

The day arrived for Jack Anderson to show us the preliminary sketches. He filled a wall with twenty-five permutations of the words: *Facèré Jewelry Salon*.

He offered the last of the twenty-five with a "ta-ta" flourish. He stood back and waited for us to agree.

The image was fine, maybe even great, but not as great as the one that was ten permutations earlier. I asked, "Will we hurt your feelings if we choose the fifteenth one, not the twenty-fifth?"

"See how it changed here," he said as if he hadn't heard me. He pointed to a slant on the letter "F" that tilted a fraction of an inch further than the one directly before it. "And we extended the *e* by a quarter of an inch."

Somehow the gradual shift wasn't persuasive. We chose and Jack was fine with the decision. Jack began the process of incorporating the logo into gift wrap, cards, sacks, and stickers.

While he did that, Don and I searched for the perfect gift box. At Northwest Box, we chose a typical jewelry box in four sizes in a plush rose color.

Years later, when we opened at Century Square with our second downtown location, we returned to Northwest Box to choose the most unique, best box ever! The salesman tried to dissuade us: "You don't want *that* box," he said with disdain. "That's a Boeing nut-and-bolt sorting box."

"How perfect!"

We promised the salesman that very box would win prizes in the world of design. And it did!

Building A Business, Building A Life

We still use that box, trimmed with a sticker, ribbon and a tie-on of pink roses.

The business card Jack designed drew the most attention. I've kept one of those beautiful cards and even today it amazes me that we had a card that was four-color, printed on two sides, embossed, and gold leafed. The cost? A dollar a card. We figured such an extravagance would never be discarded. Years later a business associate said he kept one of those cards at his desk just to admire it. He couldn't believe anyone had been so crazy.

It was time to open. The problem with one grand opening was the number of people we needed to invite. We had less than 300 square feet inside the salon. We did, however, have the lobby of the Sheraton Hotel right outside the door. In the end we divided the invitation list into three groups for three different parties: customers, friends and relatives, and President's Club members.

The President's Club, at this time, was made up of executives who promoted and grew membership for the Chamber of Commerce. Given that Facèrè was a corporation, I qualified. I was invited. Chapter Ten of this book tells how important one particular relationship made to the survival of my business!

And the parties?

We were required by our lease to order all catering services through the hotel. "Elegant" barely covers the final product: waiters in tuxedos, trays of artfully arranged hors d'oeuvres, an open bar, and a crowning touch for each event—an ice sculpture with our logo. Facèré, in ice, glowed under the pink neon Facèré sign directly overhead.

I don't remember much about the actual parties. I do remember the warm congratulations, the good wine, the toasts to success, the lovely bouquets of flowers from friends and associates. Everyone was encouraging and no one had the bad manners to mention that hotel jewelry stores are often perceived to be expensive and tasteless.

I would learn that all by myself.

CHAPTER NINE
FALLING IN LOVE WITH A SPACE

Opening night at Century Square

I didn't think I was *really* looking for another retail location.

But, I can assure you, I have never passed a space with a FOR LEASE sign in the window without imagining a new, better, exciting, and successful store. Wherever Don and I traveled, I would drag him toward the magnetic signs adorning windows: FOR LEASE—Mendocino, California; FOR LEASE—Chicago, Illinois; FOR LEASE— Ballard, Washington. It didn't matter what town or what space. I'd peer through dusty windows and I would imagine cases full of jewelry. FOR LEASE signs remain magnetic to this day.

Building A Business, Building A Life

That's how, on an evening in February, 1986, walking down Fourth Avenue on the way to see Katherine Hepburn in her one-woman show at the Fifth Avenue Theater, a space reached out. Reached out and grabbed me.

The empty space was part of a newly built office tower in Seattle on the corner of Fourth and Pike. Century Square. The building, because of its curved glass roof, would become fondly known as "the lunch-box" building.

We stood on the street admiring the entrance. A cavernous vault, leading into a thirty-foot high open space with a grand two-story escalator. Smack in the center stood a retailer's dream: a stand-alone kiosk—in the shape of a miniature lunch-box, the exact duplicate of the shape of the building. And? Paper banners with bright red letters festooned and beckoned. FOR LEASE.

Don and I ignored the "keep out" construction tape, and investigated the most beautiful retail space I had ever seen! A space as sweet and tidy as a miniature Kew Garden. Fifteen feet to a side. Twenty feet tall. Barreled cross-vault. Glass curved to fit each space. An oiled teak configuration wrapped in paper to ward off workmen's bumps and mistakes.

Don whistled a slow whistle of awe as he studied the structure. "This is a woodworker's dream. Cost to build? Sixty thousand. Fifty, minimum. In every way, fine."

He had no clue I took that as a complicit agreement to claim the space as my own.

I studied a business card discreetly taped to the

kiosk door: SPACE AVAILABLE CALL GARY CARPENTER. I pulled from my purse a pen and wrote the phone number on the back of my checkbook.

Don asked, "What are you doing?"

"Doing?" I chattered excitedly. "It's our second store! The one we've been looking for! For jewelry art! It's obvious. We can sell fine jewelry and antique jewelry at the Sheraton. We can make this a jewelry art gallery! Look, look!" I waved my arms, filling corners with cases, placing a neon sign in a window, tucking a safe in a corner. "I can't believe anything is this cute! We can do it!"

To this day, I'm amazed Don did not say, "Who is this 'we'?"

I know this momentary madness sounds a bit nuts, coming from someone who was struggling to survive at the Sheraton Hotel, but I truly was crazy-in-love and this eureka moment did make some sense.

Over the years at Facèré Jewelry Salon in the Sheraton, I had mixed manufactured jewelry, antique jewelry, and jewelry art. The large disparity between these kinds of jewelry made it difficult to define my business. I felt as if I were neither fish nor fowl nor four-footed beast. Not having a clear definition of what the store sold made advertising difficult and made restocking confusing. How does one mix computer-chip jewelry with Victorian lavalieres with diamond wedding sets?

For instance, I met Julie Spiedel through my new employee, Virginia Washburn. Julie and Virginia were running buddies. Julie, at that time (she is now a noted

Building A Business, Building A Life

Pacific Northwest sculptor), was making bold copper and brass jewelry. Virginia wore one of Julie's belts to work. It was smashing. (Julie's work was so wonderful, she had been approached by Robert Lee Morris in New York and she was on her way to becoming a major player in the world of jewelry art.)

Virginia made an appointment for me to meet Julie on an evening after work. I found my way to Julie's house in the Mt. Baker neighborhood. She welcomed me at the door and guided me downstairs to her basement where she had arranged a selection of bold and very original belts, bracelets, earrings, and necklaces. I immediately offered Julie a show.

The show was a dramatic, exciting event. The only problem was, when I showed her work, thousands of dollars worth of antique and modern fine jewelry was placed in drawers available to the customer, but not displayed in such a way as to be found easily.

Julie's show was a turning point. I loved the curved, sculptural shapes. I loved the mottled green patina. I loved how pieces reflected the hammer and the hand of the artist. The contrast between manufactured jewelry and Julie's jewelry was dramatic.

What was Facèré? The need to define what kind of a jewelry store, salon, or gallery, presented a dilemma. In the end the dilemma led to a solution. Another location.

And I had just found it! The answer to how to define the essence of Facèré resided in this small kiosk two blocks from the Sheraton Hotel. The elegant, dollhouse space at Century Square was a perfect fit. I only had to convince Gary Carpenter I was exactly who he was looking for. Gary Carpenter was about to begin a twenty-year relationship with Facèrè Jewelry Art Gallery and the world of jewelry art.

Back to that moment in 1986, the evening of the great space find. We had to get to the theatre, but, after the curtain went up, I created a budget along the edge of my program. I admit, I was totally distracted.

I whispered to Don, "How much for cabinets?"

"Ten thousand."

After a discreet time, I whispered, "How much for electrical?"

"They provide electricity."

"Lighting?"

"A thousand."

By the time Katherine Hepburn took her third curtain call, I had created a thirty thousand dollar budget. Thirty thousand just happened to match the amount of money I had in my business account. I was ready to go for broke! Shoot the Moon! All or nothing! That's what falling in love with a space can do.

The next morning I called the leasing office and miraculously got through to Gary Carpenter. He was charming, thoughtful, and appeared to be taken with my twenty-four hour dream. He suggested we meet.

Two weeks later I signed a lease.

Don designed the space including the cabinets, display cases, and a back room lab for testing gold and stones.

Three months later, we opened with a brass band, dozens of red balloons, guests in tuxedos and sneakers.

No one noticed, what with a huge crowd and everyone in high spirits, that the space was cold. Really, really cold. For the next five years from November through May, the space surrounding my beautiful kiosk was a wind tunnel of unbearably cold air.

In spite of the cold, over the years I found more and more jewelry artists. We had shows. And with every show we had a great party.

I was slowly going broke.

CHAPTER TEN
A KNIGHT IN SHINING ARMOR

Herb Bridge

Herb Bridge, the past owner and CEO of the Ben Bridge Jewelry chain, fights good causes hard and well. He founded the Seattle Better Business Bureau, he helped bring the 2000 Goodwill Games to Seattle, he served on the board of the Navy League, he chaired the American Gem Society Board of Trustees. He believes in and supports education and is known for the number of employees he has helped graduate from the Gemological Institute of America.

He has served his country well—an honored and much admired Rear Admiral in the Navy. He has served his community well—president of the Greater

Building A Business, Building A life

Seattle Chamber of Commerce (1986-1987). He co-chaired, with his son, the 2000 United Way drive. He has served on the boards of the Seattle Downtown Association, the American Gem Society, the American Legion, Kiwanis, Shriners, The American Jewish Committee, and the Federated Jewish Fund.

'Tzedakah' guides his life. Tzedakah is a Hebrew word meaning 'justice.' For Herb, the word 'justice' implies that as a member of a community it is required that one gives back to that community.

Herb Bridge would become my knight in shining armor.

On February 11, 1989, I phoned Herb and asked for fifteen minutes of his time. He responded, "Are you sure? I have a heavy schedule for the next few days."

I answered, "I'm sure. I'm about to lose my business."

His answer?

"Tell me where and when. I'll be there."

Here's why I needed to meet with Herb:

Three days before I called him, calamity had struck.

In the Sheraton Hotel Jewelry Salon, I was hanging our annual valentine competition. I stood on a step ladder, a tin valentine in the likeness of Marilyn Monroe in my hand. Kim, my manager, stepped back to say, "Yes, right there." I traded the valentine for a hammer and gave a nail a tap.

"Perfect," Kim exclaimed and at that moment everything perfect turned into everything horrible.

A short, roundish man blustered into the shop. A man in a hurry. A man full of destruction. He looked us up and down.

"Which one of you is Karen Lorene?"

The growl of his voice sent me back to third grade. Whatever I'd done, it must have been bad. He slapped an envelope on the counter. "For you," he said with a curt nod of his Brylcreemed head. Then he turned on his heel, and left.

Silence surrounded bad news. The two of us stood in front of the letter, as cautious as cats.

"You going to open it?" Kim asked.

"Eventually."

"Come on, Karen. If you don't, I will. How bad can it be?"

We could never have imagined how bad, bad can be. The letter was short and to the point.

You have thirty days to vacate the premises.

The premises was the Sheraton Hotel Jewelry Salon. The premises was an eighty-thousand dollar build-out that I had sold a piece of property to finance. The premises was my livelihood. The premises represented all of the money I had.

The news was impossible to understand. I was in the seventh year of my lease. I thought I had a lease of five years plus a five year renewable clause.

I called Howard, my attorney. I read him the letter.

"I'll get back to you," he said.

An hour later the phone rang. Howard explained there was a sentence we had missed. The lease, after five years, could be cancelled by either party without penalty.

"Do you know why this has happened?" Howard asked.

Near tears, I answered, "I haven't a clue. I've paid my rent on time. I've given all those parties. As far as I know I have great relationships with the hotel owners and the manager and the staff. How can they possibly want me to leave?"

"That's what we need to find out. Is there anything unusual going on? Anything out of the ordinary?"

I tried to think. The only thing that came to mind was the up-coming Goodwill Games. "The hotel will be the headquarters."

"That's it!" Howard exclaimed. "Someone wants your space and whoever they are, they found a way to access your lease and they have convinced the hotel they'll be a better renter than you."

"How could that be possible?"

"You're on percentage rent, right? Someone thinks they can sell more than you. Bigger items, larger inventory, bigger client base. You name it. It's a money game and they're bigger players. Hate to tell you this, but you've lost this game. Call Stephen and set up a meeting. Let me know when."

Stephen answered the phone with a laugh. "Fletcher and Associates, business consultant to the stars!" He must have seen my name on his caller ID.

It wasn't a good time for a laugh. I was weepy, scared, and angry. In a terse, clipped voice, I explained the letter and Howard's analysis.

Stephen answered, "I can't see you until next Tuesday. Spend every minute between now and then finding a new location. Plan a sale. Write the advertising copy. Set up an appointment with your banker. You're going to need a chunk of change."

My voice inched up a notch. "Stephen! Stop! We have to fight this! I'll go to the *Seattle Times! The Post Intelligencer!* I'll call all the radio stations. This can't happen." My voice dropped, "Can it?"

"It *is* happening. Don't waste your energy on anger. You're going to need every bit of strength to get you through this. I'll be there at one o'clock on Tuesday. Be ready. You're strong. You can do this." The phone went dead.

Anger consumed me: anger over my stupidity; anger over the loss of my business; anger over building out a space that would no longer be mine. For the next forty-eight hours I thought of nothing but how to destroy an unknown enemy. I couldn't stop talking. Late Sunday night, Don turned over in bed and whispered, "Enough, sweetheart. Enough. Go to sleep. Tomorrow, you plan that sale and I'll search for a new location."

Sleep evaporated. In the middle of the night I developed a plan. At eight o'clock the next morning I called Herb Bridge.

Herb arrived in leathers on his Harley. Like a god carrying thunderbolts. Like the cavalry. He strode through the Sheraton Café like the military man he is. I felt relief just watching him walk towards the booth where I waited. Herb walks military. He talks military. He thinks military. At the time he was also president of the Chamber of Commerce. He was on his way to rescue me. I could feel it.

"Good morning, Ms. Karen!" he said with a chipper voice. "You ready for battle?"

In ten minutes we had a plan.

"Call your accountant, your banker, and your business consultant. Schedule separate meetings. If all goes well, you might not even need them. But be prepared. In the meantime, I'll call the hotel publicity department and the hotel manager." Then Herb winked and said, "Then I'll call a close friend. He happens to own the Sheraton Hotel."

That's all it took. Those three phone calls. Phone calls to the right people.

By the next Thursday I had a letter of apology from the manager of the hotel. The letter clearly stated that if ever I wanted to sell my business, it would be only at my instigation. The letter also invited me and ten guests for a party in the Presidential Suite. In business, only written promises count. This counted.

To this day, I'm not sure what Herb said in those phone calls. But about three months later, having an after-dinner drink in the hotel lounge, Louis Richmond, the hotel's head of publicity and promotions, stopped by the table to ask how things were going. I answered that all was fine. And then he said, "One thing you don't ever want in this city is a call in the middle of the night from Herb Bridge."

The following week, a young woman walked into the Century Square Facèrè. She said to Mary Clare, my staff person, "I understand my cousins are buying your business at the Sheraton."

And without a blink, as sweetly as she possibly could, Mary Clare asked, "And who are your cousins?"

Mary Clare immediately called me to say, "I've found out who was after your business!"

I picked up the phone, and when the person (who I knew by accent, by reputation, and by his cousin's not keeping her mouth shut), I said, "Hi, this is Karen at Facèrè at the Sheraton Hotel. I understand you wish to *buy* my business!"

There was a huge silence. A stumbling over words, a strange response, "Oh, no, no. A misunderstanding." And then out of sheer stupidity or fear, the person said, "We do not wish to rain on your parade."

I have no idea what he meant by that, so I ended the conversation with the words, "Should you ever wish to discuss the price, let me know."

Within six months, a woman entered Facèrè Salon at the Sheraton. She was all business. She said, "I'd like to buy your location. I don't want your name, I don't want your merchandise, I just want to be in the lobby of the Sheraton Hotel."

I thought up an amount of money that would return my investment in the build-out and pay for the time and energy put into developing an identity at the hotel. Within the month I had an agreement to sell for

$50,000 down with another $50,000 over the following year at 12% interest.

Friends warned me that I'd never see the second amount.

They were wrong.

Certain people you can trust.

Certain people you can't.

CHAPTER ELEVEN
I THINK I'LL SLIT MY WRISTS

An empty Century Square

There have been times over these past forty years when the happy-calm-everything-is-great-retail-facade edges toward dissolving into a whatever-made-me-think-I-could-sell-anything-get-me-out-of-here moment of desperation. Good spirits fade under a pile of bills, lack of sales, bounced checks, impatient customers, and July rain. And in July of 1991, the emptying out of the retail stores that I shared space with at Century Square erased any semblance of good spirits. My beautiful, treasured kiosk was being left very much alone.

I began to write letters.

Even though these letters sounded aggressive and fearful, working with Gary Carpenter, one of the owners of Century Square had always been a pleasure. He was and is an honorable, fair, conscientious businessperson. We have remained cordial after all these years. The outcome, not to ruin the punch line, was positive.

I ran into Gary in the elevator about two months ago. I told him I was writing this chapter and was going to call it, "I Think I'm Going to Slit My Wrists." He answered, "Probably just about the time I was going to slit my wrists!" As it happened, he had huge retail-leasing concerns that dwarfed in the face of my small retail problem.

Our correspondence began.

July 3, 1991
Mr. Richard Clotfelter
Mr. Gary Carpenter

Dear Gary and Dick,

Three months ago at a Tenant's Association meeting I asked the tenant manager to convey to you my concern that if the businesses were headed in the direction they appeared to be, the time might come when I was the only remaining business in the corridor.
I feared I would be left "twisting in the wind."
It appears that time is getting closer and closer.

Stepping Out has been gone a month. Successful Expressions left last Saturday. Elyse at Looking Good is selling out her cosmetics to leave only a person doing nails. J. Thompson may as well be going out of business - they put a sign out every day that says, "Closing Out Sale."

I want you to know how distressed I am. The rumors have run rife. Even the cleaning staff has been overheard discussing the impending demolition of the interior space.

Bottom line: it's hell on business. In November I thought I finally had success in hand. With only one store, I would have less expense and a growing business. For the months since last November, things have been good. Each of the spring months has seen an increase in sales. With the erosion of this complex, the flat month of June feels ominous.

I want my concerns on record.

There appears to have been little, if any, effort to rent any of the retail space in Century Square since the original leasing.

I feel I am "twisting in the wind." It's time I am told something. At this stage the most I've heard is, "You'll at least be here until Christmas." Then what? What of my lease? What of the fact that I have a business that will die due to no fault of my own. To the contrary, this year alone, I have spent $75,000 on advertising (not counting Tenant's Association advertising), had two articles in the *Seattle Times* about Facèré, and brought my entire customer base to this location.

I believe I have upheld my end of the bargain. It

seems to me the honorable thing is that you let me know what is happening. I need to hear from you soon.

Sincerely,

Karen Lorene

cc: Howard Breskin, Attorney at Law

July 16, 1991
Mr. Gary Carpenter
Mr. Richard Clotfelter

Dear Gary and Dick,

Another letter.

At one point Barbara Carothers (a leasing agent Gary and Richard used for their other building, a block away, once known as Pacific First and now known as City Center) asked me to consider the possibility of leasing a kiosk space at Pacific First that would be built (this idea was presented since Pacific First opened, not during construction).

Given the non-viability of retail at Century Square, given all of the empty spaces, given the fact that I have struggled under the most adverse situation in this location with construction and then slow erosion of business, I would like to suggest we pursue the idea of moving my business to a kiosk space at Pacific First by January 1, 1992.

My business would not conflict with any other

Building A Business, Building A life

retailer at Pacific First. Who knows what kind of sales might be generated in a location that appears to have successful retail.

I realize this letter has an edge to it. My anxiety grows each day I sit over here trying to make a go of it.

I spoke with my lawyer, Howard Breskin. He says my lease clearly states Century Square is supposed to be a functioning retail mall.

I would hope there is a solution, soon, to this concern.

Please respond as soon as possible.

Sincerely,

Karen Lorene

cc: Howard Breskin, Attorney at Law

July 18, 1991
Mr. Gary Carpenter

Dear Gary,

I know that Howard Breskin, sometime in the near future, will inquire how my letters were responded to. To give us a record of what was said, and give something to help me remember, I would like to put this letter in all of our files.

In essence, I recall the conversation as follows:
- You understand how I feel about being in a space that wants for tenants.

- We have all had a difficult time recovering from the construction.
- The city has not cooperated with you on the project adjoining Century Square and has not been positive about any possibility of putting a large tenant in the center space where my kiosk is located.
- There will be an expansion of businesses in the building next door, but it will remain a two-story building.
- You have been hurt as much economically as anyone else and you and Aetna have a great incentive to make the retail space at Century Square viable.
- There are no plans to put a kiosk in the Pacific First site until the two 900 foot vacancies are filled; there was no indication from you that moving me to Pacific First was an option.
- The hope of an antique mall is premature as you have nothing in writing from the interested party nor have you seen his financials to determine if he is an appropriate person to rent the first and second floors of Century Square.
- You will keep me personally informed if anything definite should happen.
- I should write or call if I hear any other rumors or have further questions.
- You hope it will not be necessary to involve our lawyers in trying to keep my business alive.

That covers my notes from the conversation.

I made it clear, I hope, that I have no fears of surviving until Christmas. What I am most concerned about is that after the holidays, if there haven't been substantial changes (spaces filled) that I will slowly die and lose any momentum that I've been working so hard to generate.

I hung up the phone feeling you are a wonderfully pleasant person. However, I still might lose everything I've worked to create - through no fault of my own.

Sincerely,

Karen Lorene

P.S. I assume you got my message this morning concerning the reporter from the *Weekly*:
- "Does this mean you will also be leaving?"
- "I'm sorry, what do you mean?"
- "All the empty spaces, are you going to be closing also?"
- "I hope not. My business is doing so well."
- "Amazing."
- "Aren't you from the *Weekly*?"
- "Yes, I thought we might do a story on the lack of success of retail at Century Square."

That was the guts of the conversation. I suggested she call you. How many nails can anyone put in a coffin?

cc: Howard Breskin

August 3. 199
Mr. Gary Carpenter
Dear Gary,

This week's letter...

With less people at Century Square, with two bank robberies in our building in the last week, with an increase of shops being robbed on the street (Pino's, Burberry's, Trudi's, Barisof's...to name the ones I've heard of), with more people "casing our store," I am concerned for our safety.

Because of that concern and because of a particular instance when a street person frightened me last week (he crawled into my store and wouldn't leave until the police came), I have arranged a code between all of the remaining stores and the security guards at Century Square. If we call and say we need a "red file" they know they are to come to our store immediately.

As the fall days get shorter, I am concerned for my manager and myself. The last hour of the day brings very little traffic to Century Square. Because of this, I ask you to arrange for one of the guards to be on the first floor, visible to us, from 5:30 to 6:00 every day when we close.

Sales for June and July have fallen frighteningly under projections. I think the article in the *Seattle Times* hurt. I got a condolence letter from one of my customers.

Any new news about additional tenants? I have seen a number of people walking around with blue

Building A Business, Building A life

prints. Is it too much to hope that something is happening?

Sincerely,

Karen Lorene
cc: Howard Breskin

September 5, 1991
Mr. Gary Carpenter

Dear Gary,

    I'm ready to slit my wrists.

- I have just had an unpleasant exchange with the security guard, my fault, but we are on the way to an 83-degree day, I have a fan on in my store and we can't open the front doors because the computer says it's not warm enough yet.

- Betsy has just told me you have rented Dale's space to an "upscale" T-shirt shop. Great. What is an upscale T-shirt shop?

- She has told me the art glass rental has fallen through.

- The lights are off in Dale's empty space since his lease ended. We used to turn them on. I asked Betsy to have the guards take care of it. It has been dark since the first of the month. Another sign of lack of business.

- The lights are down in Successful Expressions. Betsy says the case lights are on. This is a way to save electricity?

I feel like I'm walking on quicksand. We work harder and harder to just not quite make it. It feels like a squeeze play. Please confirm that my paranoid fears of what your organization is doing to my business are unfounded. It's easy to think no one gives a damn.

Frustratedly,

Karen Lorene

P.S. Gary, I apologize for sounding so nasty. It's a combination of fear and frustration.

cc: Howard Breskin

September 9, 1991
Ms. Karen Lorene
Facèré 1501 Fourth Avenue
Seattle, Washington 98101

Dear Karen,

I am sorry you feel that we are putting a squeeze play on your business. That is certainly not the case. I have told Betsy Sutherland to turn the lights on in Dale's space and leave them on. I have also told her to make sure we override the heating and air conditioning system when we are going to have an extreme temperature day. Further, we have indeed rented Dale's former space for a short period through Christmas. We felt it was in the best interest of all tenants to have the space occupied and active during the holiday season. It is not an "upscale" T-Shirt shop. I will have Betsy drop by their concept.

We have also done a very good job of keeping art work rotating through the retail complex. The idea of an additional glass art concept in the former Successful Expressions' space was a good idea. However, none of this is guaranteed. We have been attempting to lease this space, like Dale's, on a temporary basis for the holidays. We will continue to do this.

I understand you are frustrated but please don't expect me to spin gold from straw. We also want this retail complex to work, but not everything we do is in our total control. The City of Seattle is enough of an unknown, let alone the fragile business environment we all work in.

I will continue to communicate and keep you up-to-date as to our progress on all fronts.

Sincerely,

PRESCOTT
Gary J. Carpenter
Executive Vice President

Dear Gary,

Thank you for taking time to write the letter. I realize I am a small worry in the face of all your partnership faces.

You should know that through all of this I have

never once doubted that I have the most beautiful space in all of Seattle.

Wishing us both success and fewer anxiety attacks.

Thanks,

Karen

October 23, 1991

Dear Gary,

Thank you for returning my call.

As per our conversation, I will expect to hear from you in two or three weeks concerning a proposal for my retail space in 1992.

I would like to emphasize that it is not just knowing what will happen in the next twelve to fifteen months, but whether or not Century Square in the interim is a viable retail space.

The empty spaces are a concern. I worry for our safety. My employee the other day called Security to "send the red file" down. The guard said he thought she said something about a fire and he still didn't come. It was the first time we have used the code to get the guards to us quickly. I have spoken to Security. I don't think it will ever happen again, but I can't say too strongly that being in a jewelry store in an empty mall is very scary.

Building A Business, Building A life

I hope our arrangements for the future are equitable and satisfactory. I too, do not wish to involve my lawyer, but as you can readily see, he gets copies of all these letters and he wonders what I am doing. Sorry, this truly started out as a thank-you letter.

Sincerely,

Karen Lorene

cc: Howard Breskin

And then a miracle happened…Gary Carpenter offered to build a space for Facèrè at City Centre.
Hooray! Perfect!
This is the space where Facèrè currently resides.

January 27, 1992

Dear Gary,

A quick note to say how much I appreciate your response to my requests.

Please consider it a "go" on the space. I'll get the lease back to you in the next couple of days. We will have minor clarifications similar to those on the previous lease.

Again, thank you. I could not be more pleased.

Karen

Thank goodness for miracles. Thank goodness for all Gary did to get us into our new space. What a mensch!

CHAPTER TWELVE
WHO WEARS THIS STUFF?

Where we sell our wonderful stuff

At City Centre business life changed.

The building was made for boutique businesses. Facèré was located in the very middle of the first floor with a large space which we have used again and again for openings and celebrations. Upstairs, in the office tower, we have access to an elegant and large boardroom that seats sixty-five. We regularly sponsor lectures and we always have a lecture before each show opening.

Probably the biggest change was our customer base. The number of customers increased. And the kinds of customers increased. Thanks to being surrounded by stores such as Barneys, Ann Taylor, and ROAD, customers not only shopped, but often stayed for dinner or stopped for coffee at one of the three Starbucks located in the building.

The exquisite kiosk that Gary Carpenter had built for us, and which Facèré now occupies, is as delightful and outstanding as the kiosk we had to give up at Century Square.

With the customer base changing, our selection of jewelry changed. The emphasis slowly focused on jewelry art. We have maintained a fine assortment of antique jewelry, but Facèré Jewelry Art Gallery has become known more for contemporary jewelry art than for antique jewelry. Presently we feature the work of fifty-five jewelry artists from around the world. The antique jewelry is limited, but well chosen.

It surprises me that many, many customers still haven't a clue about the world of jewelry art. Those customers ask the most confounding questions: sometimes insulting, sometimes inquisitive, sometimes serious, sometimes flattering. My answer depends on the time of day, my level of hunger, the amount of sleep I've had, or perhaps, the very jewelry I am wearing at the moment.

For instance, a customer once asked, "Do people really wear this stuff?" Stuff, of course, referred to the exceptional, exciting, beautifully made, thoughtfully constructed jewelry we show and sell (and I always wear!).

I said something like, "Yes! People wear this kind

of jewelry. Have worn it for years!" Nothing prepared me for the doubt that slipped across the questioner's brow and her eyelids narrowed in disbelief as she nailed me with, "Why?"

As I recall, I didn't get a chance to respond. The phone rang and by the time I hung up, that rude, insulting woman had left. I've never forgotten those two questions. I have practiced answers so as not to be caught off guard, but hopefully I'll never have a chance to respond to such a question again.

I've thought since about the reason people buy jewelry art. What might I have said?
- Customers buy it because it is not what their mother wore.
- Wearing jewelry art turns heads and invites comment.
- Jewelry art identifies the wearer as someone unique, interesting, even daring.
- Jewelry art isn't boring. Jewelry art is engaging.
- Jewelry art is art.

The second strangest comment, after the "stuff" question comes from the person who looks around, pulls their arms close to their side, glances sideways at a case and calls the jewelry *interesting*, as in, "This jewelry is very interesting." If the *interesting* customer stays long enough to touch a piece of jewelry, he or she will more than likely add, "Well, it would look great on you, but I'm too short, or I'm too tall, or I'm too old," at which point I spread my arms to show whatever it is I'm wearing to say, "Old doesn't count. I've passed seventy.

Our tallest customers sometimes wear the tiniest of jewelry and our shortest customer has been stopped by airport security because the necklace she was wearing was mistaken for an ammunition belt."

However, *interesting* is often the precursor to the unspoken, *I need to get out of here*! That not-to-be customer leaves. As you might guess, this was not a conversion experience.

If I am in a thoughtful mood and the potential customer's questions are sincere and the person has been pulled into the gallery because she or he has found the window displays to be confusing or intriguing or interesting or exciting or captivating or stimulating or fascinating—involvement begins. There is an identifiable energy surrounding such a customer. Our greetings to such saints are warm and instructive. We open drawers. We make "thinking trays" as they gather ideas. We remove jewelry from the case and place it in his or her hand. Should such a customer leave without purchasing, our belief is—they will return!

If a person looks around our 250 square foot shop, and says in a certain tone, "Well, you must be doing all right?" you can assume, as I do, that the statement is a question.

This observation surprises me. Facèrè is in an upscale, high-rent location. But I never know quite how to answer questions about my finances. Other questions include:
- "What did you pay for this?"
- "Is this piece consigned or did you buy it?"

Building A Business, Building A life

- "Does your husband support you?"

Amazing! I don't actually answer these questions. I say something vague, like, "We're a jewelry art gallery," and head for the front counter to rearrange anything that happens to be on the desk. Some questions don't require answers.

There are appropriate questions.

"Is this your best price?" Given the times, a customer *should* ask. Every retail establishment has its own policy. It was Kim, one of my staff, who came up with the perfect answer concerning discounting, "No. But thank you for asking." Crazy, but it works. People like to be thanked.

There is one exception to the question about finances. That exception is when another owner of a retail business asks, "How's business?" I'll share numbers, but I don't brag if we've had an exceptionally good month and I'll not be totally precise if we've had an exceptionally bad month. I choose my answers carefully. However, there is one retailer/friend with whom I share real numbers. Refreshing. Informative. We've both survived and it is helpful to learn how someone is *really* doing. I treasure that relationship.

Then there are the cherished customers. Often such a customer is a man. He doesn't ask questions. He enters the gallery with purpose. He has been sent. He has instructions, "Buy anything you want. Just buy it at Facèré." This is a much-appreciated compliment. For the men, we check what they have purchased in the past and show him what will compliment it. You see, for those men, it helps when we show them jewelry with identifiable materials: gold, silver, gemstones, so even if they think the piece of jewelry isn't quite "real" jewelry, they do what they've been told. They buy. We gift wrap. We have a happy spouse! Jewelry constructed of Legos and Barbie Doll parts are saved for another time and different customer.

Then there are the women who vary from sheepish to belligerent. They have received a gift from Facèré and they don't want it! They wonder, "What was he thinking?" We all try to remember to answer, "Let me show you the other choices your husband considered." We gather together the pieces he pondered. If all goes well, we tell her that her husband said (and only when this is the truth), "My wife is this interesting, daring woman and I'd like to give her something different. Something to match her personality." Often, the conversation doesn't get that far. The woman wants a refund.

To such women, here's my advice:

Don't return any gift of jewelry. Not because I don't wish to lose a sale, but because I can guarantee you your husband, boyfriend, or lover has sweated over this decision. You don't like his choice? Hold that thought, and put on the piece of jewelry. Right then. Wear it all day. Then wear it once a quarter. That's all he wants to see. He notices. He tells me! So, let me repeat, if you ever want to receive another jewelry gift in your entire

life, DON'T RETURN HIS GIFT, He cares. He's trying to show you how much he cares.

You, the recipient, need to come by the gallery and tell us what you *would* wear. What you *would* love. We'll put your name and your suggestions in our "Wish Book" and the next time your man comes to buy, you'll get the perfect gift. Once we've repeated this exercise over a couple of years, we will make every attempt to make the gift exactly right. And? More often than not, it is.

However, as a hedge, we remind him to say to you, "I chose this piece out of five other possibilities. If this isn't exactly right, you're welcome to exchange it." This allows you to trade and now we have on record what you like and before long you are receiving jewelry you adore! And he's chosen it.

A comment we love to hear: "Tell me about this artist's work."

We get to answer, "It is a small piece of sculpture," or "This artist's work tells a story," or "This piece allows you to bring your own story to it." At this point the word "narrative" is introduced into the showing, which is always a great thing to do because it assumes the customer is smart enough, informed enough, with-it enough to know that "narrative" is jewelry that tells a story—a tradition particularly American and particularly loved in the Northwest where we have had the pleasure and experience of being surrounded by the work of Laurie Hall, Ron Ho, Kiff Slemmons and Ramona Solberg.

Building A Business, Building A life

And then there are the customers who make their choice of jewelry in a matter of seconds. Their response is immediate. Visceral. Right. It fits their wardrobe. It fits their style. It fits their budget. "Wrap it up!" Verbal hugs all around!

A situation requiring patience is the one where the customer avoids eye contact. Without looking up they say, after being greeted, "I'll let you know when I need help." We let that person be. When the time is right, we approach that customer. Here's how that happens: the customer walks by two cases, stops, walks by another case. We are watching with a casual demeanor. We know not to intrude, but when that customer leans over a case and squints, at that moment, we are there. We open the case. We put a piece of jewelry in his or her hand. We close a clasp. We check the length of a necklace. We have broken the barrier! We are chatting. We are creating a "thinking" tray of assorted jewelry items. All in all, this makes for a great experience. Sometimes that customer buys. Sometimes that customer doesn't buy. Should the latter happen, as they depart, we hand them a card and say, "Check the web site." And they smile and you know they'll be back or their significant other will be back.

If I'm on a roll, the sun is shining, the last four customers have purchased, I'll become more directive. To the woman who for a number of reasons just can't imagine wearing jewelry art I have a passel of answers:
 - Worried about your hands not being perfect? Wear more rings.

- Feels too young? No, no, no! It's bold. Authoritative. Smart. You can do it!
- I know a woman who wears large floral earrings because her head is bald from chemo and she wears exuberant earrings because she believes the earrings replace the hair she has lost. She is absolutely right!
- No! Of course you can wear long earrings—your neck is not short, your earlobes are not over your shoulders, here look, they are much further forward. (That last sentence is *absolutely* true. It is rare, rare, rare that a person cannot wear long earrings! Go look at yourself in the mirror!
- And here is what happens to the more general, inevitable question, "Does this look good on me?" yes (we often gather the staff around the customer to vote...rule being that you must vote sincerely). If it doesn't look great, we say, "Nope!" But we also say, "Try this." And the person does and we keep going until we've found the perfect piece. No one should buy any piece of art jewelry if it is not perfect. That's our job. To find the perfect piece.

The final question: How goes the world of jewelry art? It goes well. In the last decade we have survived 9/11, the dot-com bust, and this recession. So far, so good.

After forty years I still love coming to work. Time to go!

CHAPTER THIRTEEN
ANTIQUES ROADSHOW... HOW I GOT THERE AND HOW I GOT DROPPED

Karen appraising

Chris Jussel was the first host on the American version of Antiques Roadshow.

Prior to being the host, Chris visited Seattle a number of times as a guest appraiser on KOMO Television. He invited Kathy Bailey (another local appraiser and close friend) and me to join him. We'd spend the afternoon at the station doing verbal valuations of items brought in by audience members. We enjoyed ourselves and were never stumped by not being able to identify a piece or come up with a reasonable value.

Chris came from the esoteric world of rare

furniture. My husband appraises airplanes and boats. Kathy and her husband, Paul, appraise everything, (Kathy is particularly known for her knowledge of art glass and Paul is particularly known for his knowledge of porcelains). I appraise antique jewelry. Over dinner we would share stories that saturate the world of appraising. We would also share the times we found marriages and reproductions, outright frauds, and deceptions. The strange and wonderful world of appraising is full of good stories. Antiques Roadshow did not exist. The English version did. We didn't know yet, but all that good story telling was being considered for an American television show that would soon become one of Public Television's favorite programs.

In May of 1996, I received a call from Dan Farrell.

"Karen, I'm calling from Boston. Chris Jussel gave me your name as someone who might help us on a project. Would you be able to supply us with the names of eight appraisers in your area?" He explained that he needed appraisers that could do what Chris, Kathy and I had done on the local television program. However, with enthusiasm and a hint of caution as to the demands, he said, "Our project is a bit more intense. It would involve a full day of appraising and it would attract thousands of participants."

Was I interested? Of course! I assured him I could find him as many appraisers as he needed. He promised to fax the project's details that day. Within the hour, the fax burped out a sheet with the following information:

- The program name: **Antiques Roadshow**

Building A Business, Building A life

- The producer: **Dan Farrell**
- The television producers: **WGBH Boston**
- The locations: **thirteen cities, including Seattle**
- Appraisers: **selected from auction houses such as Christie's and Skinner's, and independent appraisers**
- The host: **Chris Jussel**.

Creating the list of appraisers for Dan was an easy, pleasant task. Kathy Bailey was the first on my list. Together we discussed all of the appraisers in the area, taking into consideration a diversity of fields and the qualifications of the appraisers. I sent the list and contact information to Dan.

Shortly thereafter, invitations arrived with information:
- Costs of travel would be the responsibility of each appraiser.
- No compensation would be paid for appraising.
- Each appraiser would NOT attempt to purchase items from the attendees.
- Each appraiser was required to attend a training session on Friday, August 9, at three o'clock at The Convention Center.
- Appraisers would report at eight o'clock Saturday, August 10, and work until five-thirty.
- We could bring business cards which would be on a table at the door where attendees could pick them up.
- We should dress professionally.

- Fingernails were to be clean and trimmed.
- Should we have the opportunity to be televised, a make-up person would be provided.

I'm not sure about the other appraisers, but I spent the summer months delving into my library. I went from moments of feeling totally prepared to moments of panic. How could I have ever dreamed I was capable? Then I'd remember the afternoons with Chris and calm down. I'd been in the business for twenty-some years. I'd studied conscientiously. I'd gone to Jewelry Camp. I'd sponsored three national weekend conferences on antique jewelry in Seattle. I'd done dozens of appraisals. I could do it!

Then came August 9. Fearful and ecstatic, I arrived a half hour early at the Convention Center. At the entrance to the main room of the center, I showed my driver's license and received my name tag. Fresh coffee was available in the back corner.

The room was filled with cameras, wires, tables, crew. The edge of the room was surrounded with six-foot draped tables behind which were the Antiques Roadshow banners: TOYS, GLASS, FURNITURE, FINE ART, PORCELAIN AND POTTERY, PAINTINGS AND PRINTS, WATCHES AND CLOCKS, DOLLS, MUSICAL INSTRUMENTS, PRIMITIVES, GLASS. And of course, JEWELRY.

The appraisers gathered for instruction. Dan Farrell, clip board in hand, took over the training session.

We were to look for the unusual, the interesting, the learning situation, the surprise reveal, in other words, we were to "find the story."

Once we had a great candidate with a good story we were NOT to disclose that the piece, for whatever reason, might be chosen to be filmed. Especially if the value was exceptional, we were not to tell that "surprise" until the end of the interview. The camera needed to capture the surprise, the joy, even the sadness. This was television!

Dan gave us some general rules to follow:
- Once we were convinced we had something television worthy, we were to find him or his assistant.
- We needed to "pitch" the story in two or three minutes.
- If the "pitch" was successful, he would return with the appraiser to convince the person to be filmed.
- A make-up person would prepare both the attendee and the appraiser.
- And never, ever, were we to give away the value until the end of the interview to give the viewers a surprise ending!

It was time to practice.

For two hours, we took turns rehearsing while Dan watched. One of us would be the owner of the item and the other person would be the appraiser. Everyone got into the spirit of "story telling" and with a non-descript item in hand, the pretend attendee would explain that it was hundreds of years old, found in a tomb in Peru, brought by smugglers to San Francisco, traded for pure gold.

The practice session was good fun. Facing the next day's reality, appraisers became serious with no encouragement. The pretend attendees worked at making the interview entertaining and difficult:

"Why don't you think this piece is from Peru?" Said with great consternation by the pretend owner of the pretend antique piece.

Appraiser: "The marks on the bottom, these four impressions, are clearly British."

"My grandmother got this from her grandmother. It's probably even older than that!" Said with conviction.

Appraiser: "Look carefully at the clasp on this brooch. It was patented in 1901."

"Are you sure?" Said with total skepticism.

Appraiser: "My associates at the jewelry table and I examined the piece carefully." Then with a smile and a slight touch of the hand, "This piece is one of three! The other two are in the British Museum and the Smithsonian! Have you any idea of its value? No? Well, hold on to your hat! (The pretend-attendee grabs her head.) It would sell at auction for one million dollars!"

Dan: "Maybe a few less exclamations."

And so the afternoon continued.

After the practice session, we were shown the rooms behind the curtains. One area was given over to a library and computers. The lunch room was to be used at our discretion (quickly). In the make-up area we saw that there were plenty of creams and jars to do the job. The next day there would be a make-up artist. One area was designated the "green room" and was

Building A Business, Building A life

generously supplied with magazines and newspapers for those waiting to get on camera.

At the conclusion of the tour, Dan Farrell ended the day by explaining the best way to pitch to him:

- Give him the most important details first.
- Condense the "story" into a single sentence.
- Tell him the single best reason the piece should go on television.
- If he says, "No," he means, "No, thank you," and there is no further discussion.

His final suggestion was to consult with the other appraisers at our table. We were all chosen because we were professionals and we would be the best source for each other, for checking values, checking authenticity, and getting the best information for the camera. He reminded us, Antiques Roadshow was going to be a wonderful service, but we were never to forget that the show needed to capture the audience.

One final word: Dan assured us that if we made a word or a date mistake, that mistake could be corrected. And, should we get home and realize what we had said on camera was not on target, we were to call and request the piece be cut. They did not want us to look stupid. They did not want the show to look stupid.

And so ended the first day.

Seven-thirty the next morning I was at the Convention Center with an armful of books on antique jewelry. I'd also brought an extra loupe, price guides, and a stack of two hundred business cards.

When we had all arrived, the jewelry table was staffed with Barry Weber, Gloria Lieberman, Ted Irwin, a Seattle appraiser, and me. I'd met both Gloria and Barry at Jewelry Camp in Maine. It was reassuring to know that, given their extensive knowledge, I would be able, should I need it, to ask for extra help.

Then the doors opened!

All day the lines in front of every table remained constant. At the appraisal table, I was pleasantly surprised by my competence. My years in the business paid off. Only twice did I have to hand a piece of jewelry to Gloria (sitting directly to my left). One brooch was a signed Cartier; a platinum brooch encrusted with diamonds and emeralds. The piece was beyond my ability to appraise. Another time I was stumped by a large costume clip. Once again, Gloria graciously accepted it and I immediately returned to the dozens and dozens of people waiting in line.

My confidence grew over the next five years of doing the show. For those eight hours each day, I came to yearn for the unusual and rare. Most jewelry was not demanding. Most jewelry was of the type I had appraised dozens of times: cameos, rock crystal necklaces, filigree rings and necklaces from the 1920s, rose gold jewelry from the 1940s, and jet and vulcanite from the 1890s.

Once or twice a day, someone would approach with a "worthy" item. I'd casually say, "I'll be right back" and run to find Dan.

With one such item I found Dan in the crowd, waited until he was free of other appraisers "pitching" and then I said, "I've got it! This bracelet is her grandmother's, a minister's wife. The grandmother had

Building A Business, Building A life

to cut the necklace into pieces so as not to look too "showy!" Value around $3000 if it were restored!"

"That's it?" Dan asked.

"Nope! Here's the good part. She has a second piece she just purchased. She was told it was Victorian. It's a reproduction! It's a good story/bad story."

Hooray! Dan said yes.

It didn't always happen that way. I had a person with a rare gold necklace that had belonged to Martha Washington. She had the documentation. Fabulous! Selling Dan was a snap! Dan approached the woman and she answered, "No thank-you. I don't want to be on television." Dan tried persuading her with an argument that the piece would be very educational. "No!" She thanked us, placed her necklace in her purse, and left.

To this day I think that was a first for the Roadshow. It broke my heart.

After the wonderful experience in 1996, I waited anxiously for the next summer's information. On a cold, crisp day in January, 1997, a letter arrived. In the corner was the return address: WGBH Boston. I tore open the envelope and was greeted with the words, "Welcome back." I had been invited for the 1997 summer tour. The invitation listed ten cities. I chose Denver and San Francisco.

For the following four years I always chose two cities. Two trips away from Facèré was what I budgeted. Travel, hotel, and time away cost approximately $1500 a weekend. Had I been financially able, I would have signed up for all of the cities and let the assignment person at the Roadshow place me where they wished. But what if they chose a weekend I had scheduled for my Great Books Conference or a trip home to Spokane or the weekend I attended the writers' conference at Centrum?

Kathy Bailey's strategy was to choose all ten cities. She made herself available. Kathy is a spectacular appraiser and she put her business first and the Roadshow first. She is still a regular on the Roadshow.

Life had its way of interrupting my love of the Roadshow. The worst interruption was on July 7, 1999. I had my airplane ticket; I was ready to leave for Salt Lake City the next morning. The phone rang and my brother had the horrific, unexpected news that our father had died. I called the hotel in Salt Lake and told Dan they would have to count me out.

In 2000 I was in San Diego and St. Louis.

In 2001 the two cities I chose were cancelled by the Roadshow.

In 2002 I had no free weekends except for the weekend the show came to Seattle. I was recovering from minor surgery to my face. Because of the swelling, I handed any item that had a good story to one of the other appraisers. I wasn't ready for prime time.

The following year I was not invited. Dear, sweet Kathy tried to remind the powers that be that I was still interested, but for whatever reason, I no longer received that wonderful list of cities in January.

Then in the summer of 2007 I got an urgent phone call. The very next weekend, Antiques Roadshow needed a jewelry appraiser. One of the jewelry appraisers was ill. Would I fly to Tucson? I wanted to say "Yes." I know the producer found it unfathomable, but I replied, "Sorry. I have a dinner party this weekend. A dinner party I can't cancel."

A dinner party?

A very important customer and her husband were flying in from Washington D.C. She was and still is a major collector. Her husband was a past member of the National Security Council. Over time we had become friends. This dinner had been planned for two months. There was no way I could call and say, "Oh, no dinner. I have to be on Antiques Roadshow." As I write this I think maybe they would have understood. I didn't take the chance.

There have been no more Roadshow invitations.

I love the show.

I watch it faithfully.

CHAPTER FOURTEEN
THE WRITING BUSINESS

Karen's first publishing adventure

In 1986 I hired a two-person advertising agency. The owner of the agency suggested I write a book. I thought he meant a book with pages and an index and paragraphs. He didn't. He meant a booklet, something like an expanded brochure. He didn't realize that he was talking to someone who admires Sisyphus.

For the next six months, I arrived early at Facèré Salon in the Sheraton Hotel. I headed for the employee's cafeteria. For two hours I wrote. When I finished, I had written *Buying Antique Jewelry: Skipping the Mistakes*.

Next, I hired an editor. Then I hired a photographer. My goal was to have a book finished, in hand, and ready to sell by February, 1987. That February I was to speak to the National Association of Jewelry Appraisers in conjunction with the Tucson Gem Show. I had six months to get the book published. Surely I'd find a publisher in that amount of time.

I knew nothing about agents or editors and the route to getting a book published. The one publishing house I sent the book to rejected it! I was dumbfounded. How could it be rejected?

Naïve? Indeed. But determined. One rejection was enough. I checked the yellow pages. I found a local book publisher on 80th Avenue. I drove north and handed over my finished copy. The deposit was two thousand dollars. I wrote the check. They guaranteed me a delivery in time for Tucson! Hooray! This was more like it.

Somehow, in my excitement, I never added up the costs: the photographer, the editor, the printer. When the final bill arrived 1000 copies cost me $11,000! Astounding. Every time I sold a book at wholesale, which was more often then selling the book at retail, I lost three cents.

But, I had my book. I was an "author."

In the end the cost was worth every penny. Speaking engagements increased. The book led to a certain authority in the world of antique jewelry. Being an author helped when I was approached by the producers of Antiques Roadshow.

I had combined two passions: jewelry art and writing. If *Buying Antique Jewelry: Skipping the Mistakes* was a joy to write, I thought writing fiction would be even more fun.

I called the College of Arts and Sciences at the University of Washington. I already had two degrees; surely they'd want me to get a third. One problem: to get a writing degree, I'd have to take the graduate exam and I would not be able to enroll until fall—an entire year away. My impatience must have carried over the phone because the woman at the administration office suggested I check into The Certificate Program. The classes in this program are scheduled for evenings and attract serious writers, but writers who have day jobs and want to start writing immediately. I enrolled.

In the Certificate Program, I took every class offered, except for Advanced Screenwriting. Screenwriting dropped by the way-side because of an incident that occurred at my first class. The instructor, Stewart Stern (whose claims to fame include writing the screenplay for *Rebel Without a Cause* and *Rachel, Rachel*), invited his best friend, Sydney Pollack to spend the day with our screenwriting class. Pollack flew to Seattle in his private airplane and spent the day with our class. His first question was, "Who expects to make a living as a screenwriter?" Every hand attached to every student under twenty-five years of age went into the air. He suggested the class move to Los Angeles. With that show of hands, I realized screenwriting was not the route I would follow.

I did however take all of the other classes offered in the Certificate Program: Fiction, Non-Fiction, and Poetry. After finishing the classes at the University of Washington, I found a private class with a brilliant teacher by the name of Priscilla Long, and have been enrolled in her classes ever since.

The classes also led to a writing group. The group—Super Group, has been meeting weekly, except in the summer, for the past seventeen years.

That's how writing became half of my life. I've written dozens of short stories and three novels. I have had a few pieces published. I won a small writing award. I loved every minute.

Writing led to Facèré creating *Signs of Life*, a literary magazine, which has been published for seven years. Each year, the Facèré staff helps choose nine jewelry artists to create new work for the show. One piece from each artist appears in the publication. I invite nine published writers to "bounce off" of an assigned image. We have had poets, novelists, essayists, and short-story writers write for *Signs of Life*.

The pleasure of producing this literary magazine led to the publication of another book titled *Celebrating 70*, published in 2010. This book features seventy jewelry artists. Each artist agreed to create one piece of jewelry commemorating a single year for the past seventy years. In addition, the artists had twenty-five words to describe their inspiration for their artwork. The book was published with Blurb, a company that is a pay-per-print publisher. The profit on each book is the goodwill and publicity it has garnered. Facèré and the *Celebrating 70* reception were featured in *Ornament Magazine* and *The Seattle Times*. News of the book and reception were included in the blogs/newsletters of *American Craft, Wired Jewelry, Art Jewelry Forum, Lark Books*, and *Klimt02*. Everyone should have so much fun on their 70th birthday!

Another recently published book (2011), *ABeCeDarian*, grew from a jewelry art show based on the alphabet. It's a small book, for children and adults filled with color photos of the alphabet jewelry and extravagantly rich alphabet words. It was written for all the children I never had.

Writing *Building a Business* is another facet of my writing/publishing adventure. One more reason for a party—to launch this book!

Do love those parties. Do love this writing.

CHAPTER FIFTEEN
STAYIN' ALIVE, STAYIN' ALIVE

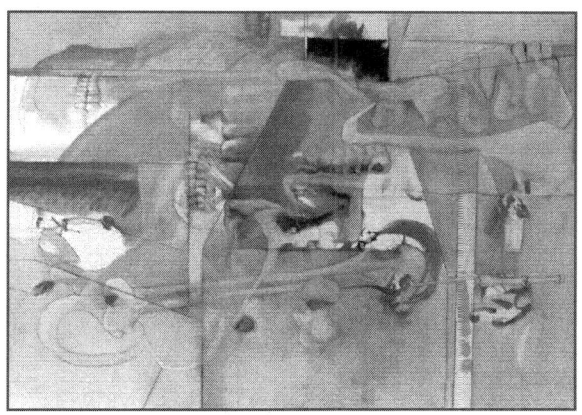

One of Karen's 4x6 foot paintings

There's more to life than business. There are eight hours for sleep. There are six hours for work. There are ten more hours. All work and no play, you know the end of that story.

Filling time when you are single is a challenge. Dear friends took me under their wing. Mary and Lou Michaelson had belonged to a Great Books group for about twenty years (I have now been a member for over 30 years). Great Books grew out of the University of Chicago, when Robert Hutchens and Mortimer Adler placed their mark not only on the university, but on the nation. In 1947 they had a dream of creating meaningful discussions around great literature. A foundation was established. Readers were turned into discussion leaders through sponsored workshops across the country. A group was founded in Seattle, Washington. Mary and Lou thought I might enjoy a night out once a month for the sole purpose of a two-hour, keep-to-the-text literary discussion.

For the first meeting, the reading was *Hunger* by Knut Hansen. I went to the library. I checked out every book available by Hansen. I read seven books. A bit over-prepared, but I was new to the group and I was new to the process.

I fell in love with the Great Books members, procedures, and literature. I needn't have read everything by Knut Hansen, but it didn't hurt. I think the members of the group saw that I was serious about being a participant. (Rule number one of Great Books is that you are not allowed to join in the discussion if you haven't read the book.) Where else would I have had the opportunity to discuss Thucydides' *Peloponnesian Wars,* Plato's *The Republics,* Aristotle's *Poetics and Politics?* And if you think it is all work and no play; the group also read Erica Jong's *Fear of Flying.*

Lou and Mary were also the reason I became addicted to the theatre. They introduced me to ACT when the theatre was located at the bottom of Queen Anne Hill. The seating on the right hand side was pie shaped. The pie shape ended in a single seat. Front and just to the right of center. The first row. The only seat.

That was my seat the first night I attended theatre

with Lou and Mary. I felt like Hester Prynne. Right out of *The Scarlet Letter*, with an "A" on my forehead for ALONE. (Mary and Lou had middle, center seats.) But after that first performance of *When You Coming Back Red Rider?* I was hooked. That front row, single seat was mine. For as long as ACT was at that location, I paid for that particular seat. It was as if the play was created just for me! To this day I love the magic of live performances.

I learned to ski when I was thirty. I know no one else but me who spent an entire year on the bunny hill. I became a very good skier on the bunny hill. I loved the gentle slope and gentle skiing. No one ever told me I should try the chair. It was another example of Dewey's "learn by doing." The next year at Snoqualmie Pass I was ready! I became a "hell bent for leather" skier.

Rain in Seattle in winter often means snow in the mountains. I loved the rain. The rain augured well for someone who had fallen in love with downhill skiing.

Twenty years later I skied for the last time at Sun Valley. I rented equipment. The boots and new short skis were perfect! Instead of returning them to the rental, I purchased them. The season was over, but I was ready for the next year. Well, not quite ready. In August Dr. James Crutcher, my orthopedic surgeon, informed me it was time to have a hip replacement. He scheduled the surgery for February. The following November I had the second hip replaced. The doctor's answer to my plaintive question: "Sure you can ski. I'll just see you sooner."

How I miss that thrill of going down hill. Straight. Fast. On the very edge of losing control. Delicious.

I've taken that attitude once in awhile in my business. Like spending $6000 per ad on our "Women Who Make a Difference" campaign. Or, publishing a book that costs more to produce than the final price.
Delicious.

It took eleven years of morning classes to get my Bachelors of Fine Arts in painting. I took one class a quarter. By eleven o'clock I would be at work. By the time I was near graduating, two of my instructors, Bob Jones and Mike Spafford, encouraged me to apply for a Rome Prize. I didn't win (the year I applied the winners were Robert Motherwell, Joyce Carol Oats, Robert Venturi....whatever happened to the emerging artist concept, I have no idea).

In preparation for applying for the Rome Prize however, I created a portfolio. When I knew I wasn't headed for Rome, I prepared to approach local galleries in Seattle.

I made a list of the galleries I would most like to be represented by. At the top of the list was Foster White. They accepted me.

I had my first show. The show sold out. I was in heaven!

However, in less than two years, Don Foster hired a new gallery director. Her first job was to clean house. Fifteen artists were dropped. I was one of them. It took my breath away. I even asked for a private meeting with Don Foster. I promised him I could sell

Building A Business, Building A life

out another show. Given my retail experience, I had no doubts I could accomplish such a feat. His answer was that he would not cross his gallery director.

I was crushed. For awhile I had an agent, Diane Hill, to represent my work. But the joy had been knocked out of me, and just about this time, my business consultant suggested I might want to pay a bit more attention to business.

Two paintings hang in my house and I admire them as if they were painted by someone else. I like being reminded that once I was a painter.

The need to create through painting has been replaced with working on writing skills. Probably, a good move as I had become quite addicted to breathing turpentine. Love the smell of turpentine in the morning!

When North Country Fair was sold to the Smuggler Restaurant, I had a chunk of money. I paid all my bills. The chunk was getting smaller. Before the money disappeared, I decided to take a trip to Europe. I told my (ex) husband I was going to go and he was more than welcome to come with me.

And so we took our first trip to Europe. It was the typical first adventure of sixteen cities in twenty-one days. It was a great introduction to travel. Since then I've been back a number of times and have fallen crazy in love with Italy.

Don and I joined a cooking tour with twenty other people in Oaxaca and then the next year we joined the same group for cooking lessons in a villa outside Luca.

In May of 2010 we rented a six-foot wide, sixty-

five-foot long canal boat in England with family.
Next? Can hardly wait. I think it will be Machu Pichu.

I have always loved to read. Most anything. Most everything. I read Tolstoy at a much too young age. I read *Winnie the Pooh* at a much too old age. I just finished a two-inch-thick biography of the Mitford Sisters. There are six boxes of books in storage (they don't fit on the houseboat – too heavy), that have never, ever, been opened. I need to live a long, long time to finish reading all the unread books. It's reading that led me to writing that led me to publishing. I only wish I had seventy more years to get to all that waits.

I have also experienced the joy of physical work. After separating from my first husband, I chopped wood. I had just under an acre of land. I had lots of wood. Chopping took the place of thinking, worrying, wondering. You need to take your mind off of divorce? Chop wood.
Besides chopping wood, I took up running. I always thought I would run a marathon. I did a half-marathon at Marymoor Park, and about three-quarters of the way through the course I knew I'd never run a marathon.
I continued to run 10K's. My artificial hips now preclude any running.
Sometimes I think if I'd put the energy into swimming or water aerobics, I might still have my own hips. Strange how we do things thinking they are healthy for us, and then we wonder.

And my greatest love? Don. We're crazy about each other. Still.

CHAPTER SIXTEEN
ARTISTS AND WHERE THEY COME FROM

One of our most beloved artists, Ramona Solberg

Once, after a Society of North American Goldsmiths' (SNAG) conference, standing in line at the airport, a young man in line with me turned to say, "Saw you at the conference. Are you a jeweler?"

"No, I'm a gallery owner."

"Oh, that's too bad."

"Bad?"

"Yeah, I'm a jeweler. I wouldn't show with a gallery again if you paid me."

"Why, what happened?"

"Well, besides the fact that they didn't pay me until I inquired, they never, ever let me know how I was doing. I never knew if they sold stuff. It was horrible.

"And, if a gallery changed their ways? Would you reconsider?"

"I doubt it. I was burned. All the artists talk about how they are burned. Why don't gallery owners know? You're not very well thought of as a group."

I was astounded. I didn't know.

When I returned from the conference, the staff and I began to address the problem of communication. We send out quarterly statements. We make a point of having checks out exactly on the thirtieth of each month. Without fail. We email artists the minute we receive work or we return work. We produce an electronic newsletter each month and request of our artists news of their achievements. We are still learning ways to stay in touch and we encourage artists to be in touch with us, for whatever reason.

A question we are asked most often is: "Where do you get your artists?"

Truth is, I don't "get" them. We more often than not stumble upon each other. For instance, the summer of 2011. I spent two days in Twisp, Washington. One of the boards I serve on, Artist Trust, met there for their summer board meeting. As we gathered, I noticed a spectacular bracelet on the arm of one of the board members.

"Very fine!" I said.

She answered, "Just bought it. Across Main Street. The jeweler owns the gallery."

By the end of the day I could hardly wait to see

more of her work and was pleased when entering the gallery to see there was a large selection. The materials and design were absolutely fresh and original. I asked and was immediately led to the artist/owner of the gallery.

I introduced myself and told her how much I admired the originality of her pieces.

"Well, thank you. Glad you like it. Only thing, it's older work. I'm no longer producing anything like it. In fact, I'm mostly doing commissioned work."

"Any chance you could be convinced to reconsider?"

"My husband is up for traveling. I'm cutting back."

I didn't give up immediately. "The work is very exciting. Very fresh. Even if you created it awhile ago. It's great!"

"Thanks," and then she repeated what she had just said. No question, she was saying "no."

It was hard to give up. I gave her my card and invited her to check out the web site. "In case you change your mind."

She thanked me, but the conversation ended.

I was totally sold on her work. I think if by a miracle she does change her mind, her work would be a great addition to Facèrè. I suspect this arrangement will never happen.

I found her at the wrong time. But the door is always open.

Serendipity is part and parcel to finding jewelry

Building A Business, Building A life

artists. Finding artists is like going fishing. Sometimes you come home empty handed. Sometimes you aren't even in the boat, didn't have any bait, or a fishing pole, and you still get the fish!

Here's a time when everything was a "yes!"

I was in Cleveland, Ohio for a SNAG conference. The schedule for the gallery crawl led to a studio where the Lark Ring Show was on display. The show was traveling to our gallery in a couple of months and it was important to see how it was displayed, and how we might display it. There were approximately 250 rings. The show was great.

Then magic happened. I walked by a jeweler's bench tucked into the corner of the studio. On the bench, in the middle of being assembled, were tiny discs of patinaed silver with bright splashes of gold and up-side-down set diamonds (reverse set diamonds).

"Whose work is this?" I asked a small group of artists standing near by. One person indicated a young fellow on the other side of the room busy showing rings from the Ring Show.

I waited. I continued to wait. This person was worth waiting for.

Finally he was free and I approached him.

"I've been looking for you for two years!" I exclaimed. His work was small, discreet and powerful. It was exactly the niche we had not filled at Facèrè.

Todd Pownell was interested. Within a month he had work to us. We began selling immediately.

Today Todd is one of our best sellers. He is a pleasure to work with. He keeps inventing new designs.

He keeps us well supplied.

It wasn't even a fishing trip and I came home with a perfect catch!

Artists sometimes appear miraculously. They happen. They descend. They turn up. They confront. Or, they make appointments, email, send discs, actually write a letter. Or, he or she walks into the gallery to see a show or visit the work of another artist. He or she does one thing that every jewelry artist should do. They wear their jewelry!!

Approaches vary. It is rare when we take on a new artist. But it happens.

Sometimes these different approaches lead to a contract. Sometimes, no matter how perfect the approach, nothing happens.

There's no formula.

Artists should always take a chance.

Even when I think I'm not looking, when I believe I can't possibly accommodate a new artist, the right one comes along. Presto! It's magic! And we have a new artist.

CHAPTER SEVENTEEN
CUSTOMERS AND A BIT MORE

Facèré lecture filled to capacity

About customers: They come in every shape and size, they come in good moods and bad moods, and customers come on a mission or on a search. Then there is the customer who wanders through the gallery because he has just left the divorce attorney on the twenty-second floor who has said, "No, the diamond engagement ring that belonged to your grandmother will not be returned, ever," and that customer looks at the jewelry in my gallery with pure, unadulterated anger and silently swears, never, ever again, no matter what, to give a piece of jewelry to anyone for any reason! Ever! Never!

Building A Business, Building A life

Given the human condition, I believe, someday he will change his mind and find a reason to return to Facèré.

Given all the different customers, some who we love and some who we don't love, some who we are pleased to see because they have become friends, and some who we have no feelings about, because she or he, for the moment, only needs directions to the bathroom. But just in case the individual who is headed for the bathroom and who might someday need a special, unique piece of jewelry, we have been known to call to his or her back, "When you need jewelry, remember us!"

You see, I believe, as I was taught forty years ago by Joe Miller, a fast-talking, speed-selling vacuum-cleaner salesman, "Everyone is a potential customer." He also told me he'd sold a thousand vacuum cleaners in 1972 because he believed his selling floor was his living room, and anyone coming into his living room was a friend, or was going to be a friend. And certainly anyone in his living room where he sold vacuum cleaners wouldn't mind hearing about a unique, beauteous, wonderful vacuum-cleaner.

Remember the story of the farmer who comes to the car dealership in his overalls and gum boots and no one pays him any attention? He gets attention when he raises his voice to say, "I want that one!" and the salesmen at the water cooler still look skeptical until the farmer opens a paper bag and takes out bundles of bills.

American myth? Perhaps. But here's a true story:

Building A Business, Building A life

V visited a very, very high-end department store in San Francisco wearing a muumuu and tennis shoes. She approached a clerk. She opened her purse. She took out the store's catalogue. She pointed to the front page. "I'd like to see this brooch, please." And the clerk said with raised eyebrows and flared nostrils, "Well, you know that piece is $64,000."

V looked at him with astonishment. And then she said with a bite to her words, "And you know, young man, I could buy your whole damn store if I wanted, so go get me that piece of jewelry."

We have never underestimated V. Especially after she told us this story.

We love to see her coming!

The lesson? All of us at Facèré are aware that many customers do not look as if they have ever worn a piece of jewelry, let alone purchased a piece of jewelry. We try to remember to be kind and attentive to everyone who passes through our "living room." Because who knows when it's going to be V?

So, here are six of our most outstanding customers.* And to keep this chapter on a positive note and to keep you reading to the very end, let me tell you about customers who are the very, very best and about one customer who isn't. A qualifier: some customers have money; some customers have little to no money. Whether one is a good customer or a bad customer, has little to do with money.

Let's start with D. D loves jewelry that is controversial. She purchases jewelry that demands attention: a bandolier that looks like a terrorist's ammunition belt, a Viagra and birth-control pill necklace, a ring made from the trigger of a gun, a Barbie Doll necklace made of two dozen Barbie arms. Presently she is considering a necklace made from X-ray film of a woman who had breast cancer.

She loves to tell the story of being stopped at the airport in her bandolier necklace. She explained to the attendant, "It's a necklace." He was having none of it! "It doesn't look like a necklace! It looks like a gun belt." She agreed. It took another hour and another half-dozen attendants, but she finally caught her plane. This incident happened some years ago. Today she'd probably still be in detention.

D buys jewelry that probably no other person in the world would buy. We call her when the most outrageous pieces arrive. Sometimes she doesn't buy, but we are always glad to see her because she appreciates the edge of our world. She understands the edge of our world. Wherever she goes people ask her about what she wears. Her life is full and rich and she has a laugh like a peeling bell. No question, we love her.

Mr. I arrives twice a year. When he walks through the door, I think, "The marines have landed!" He is, in fact, an ex-marine. He walks like an ex-marine. He talks like an ex-marine. You can't sweet-talk him into anything. His descent on our gallery has been going on for twenty years. He has an eye for the very best in Victorian jewelry. He moves through the gallery. He needs to be left alone for about six minutes. He will pay attention if I point out something small and discrete which his eye might not have caught (but that is very, very rare). By the end of ten minutes he has chosen the pieces of jewelry he wishes to buy. "That one. And that one." He hands me his charge card. We always get a REJECTED, PLEASE CALL notification on his charge card. All year he buys gas with this card and then on this single occasion, his charge jumps one-hundred fold. He is always irritated with the card company. He, in his marine voice, tells them they do this every year. Finally they approve of his charge. We wrap each package with special care. And then? Then we talk about his airplanes. I catch him up to date on my husband's experimental airplane (recently replaced by a boat). We talk boats and airplanes and hips (we both share replaced hips). I love this customer because he is decisive. And he is fun. I'll see him again. In six months.

Every holiday season, H and J come bustling into Facèré, out of the cold, ready to shop! The energy in the gallery goes up fifty percent. They are full of good cheer. They have news about the world of writing. Successes and more successes. And I tell them yes, I'm still working on it (the writing). After the greetings and ritual catching-up, we know the two of them will begin the process of their holiday shopping. The gift is for her. We let them meander. They check every case. They check every drawer. Once in awhile, we'll pull from understock something they might not have seen. Once in awhile we introduce them to the newest work that has arrived for the holidays. We create a "thinking" tray of items that are under consideration. Eventually they have five to ten pieces that have caught their attention. They discuss each piece. She tries on each piece. Then? She leaves. To go have a cup of coffee. H chooses her holiday gift. J never knows which one he will choose. His choice is the surprise! We wrap, chatting all the time about books and awards and his latest success and then he is out the door to go find his lovely bride. H and J make the season bright!

We have a customer who now brings her grandchild to shop with us. She reminds me of my mom. I always want to give her a big hug when she comes in the door, but it's not appropriate, so I give her lots of attention. S has purchased from us for over thirty years. She is very particular. She brought her teenage granddaughter in about a month ago, and I thought it would be one of those generational disputes where they would not see eye to eye on anything. It happened that the first thing S pointed out to her granddaughter was a "No, that's not for me," but then, as they worked their way through the cases, they found five pairs of earrings that they both found "interesting." They both tried on each pair.

Grandma was concerned that people would look at her neck. I assured her that with great earrings, people would look at her great earrings. Granddaughter couldn't make up her mind between two pairs. And of course, Grandma bought both and bought the great earrings for herself. I told the granddaughter, "You've got such a great grandma," and she agreed. Much as I was tempted I didn't give either one of them a hug goodbye.

Building A Business, Building A life

And then there are the kids. Realize "kids" are almost anyone looking at wedding rings. Maybe it's the momentousness of the occasion, but couples looking for wedding rings have "young" written all over them. They are special. Focused. Nervous. Undecided. They arrive with a multitude of expectations and a shifting budget. What they need most? They need to "play."

We encourage, no, we insist, they try on many, many rings. They need to know what feels best. They need to look in the mirror as if they are looking at a different person. They need to feel the weight of the ring and they need to adjust to the "bling" of the ring (which ranges from a little to a lot). They need appropriate information about the diamonds (we have a 3x5 card with information from an independent appraiser because they need to remember what they have looked at, tried on, and considered).

In the middle of the playing, they begin to narrow the choice of rings and face the reality of the budget. Budget is a trick. Many a partner indicates money will not be discussed in front of their intended. An equal number of couples have previously agreed on the exact budget. The fun part about budget is reassuring the couple that "two months of his salary" was a slogan made up by an advertising department by someone who probably would never, ever spend two months of his or her salary on a wedding ring.

We have wedding rings from $97 to $16,000. I've assured more than one couple that they will be smarter to take a honeymoon to Europe in lieu of a wedding ring they can't afford.

Every couple has their expectations and every couple has their limits. Together we figure out a match.

And then there is the miserable customer. Horrible. The worst. Do they know? Never. They haven't a clue. That customer is crazy. Nuts. Insulting.

It is not true that the customer is always right. C was wrong! Really wrong!

C descended upon Facèré with tension, anger, fear, outrageousness, insults. Steaming. She stomped up to the counter. She banged her hand on the top of the case. She demanded to see the owner. (I wasn't there...this is a twice-told-tale.) Her hands shook. Her eyes were wide and unblinking. She could barely open the black gift box in her hand. When she finally got the box open, she pointed at the single stud earring nestled in the black foam. She leaned into the space separating my staff person from her outrage. She snarled, "There! See that? Gone! The earring is gone!" Without saying another word, my staff person got the message. We were expected to replace that lost earring. At no cost! (No cost to her.) My salesperson smiled. She took a deep breath. She held the gift box with its lone occupant in her hand like a precious treasure. She looked directly at the customer, and said in a low, controlled voice, "Tell me your story."

The customer purchased a pair of earrings in February. It was now April. She had called the jewelry artist who made the earrings to say that one of the earrings was lost and it was his fault. How so? It fell off. Now, we are speaking of a stud earring with a friction back. A normal everyday earring. He told her that he

Building A Business, Building A life

had used these very same backs for fifteen years and no one had ever called to tell him that the earring fell off because of him. In fact, he had never had any one else call him about ever, ever losing an earring. C insisted there was a defect in the earring. The jewelry artist told her he'd get back to her after he spoke to his gallery.

Which he did. I agreed with the artist to replace the earring at cost. One-half of the original cost of one earring. I called the customer. She wasn't there. I left a message. She wrote to say she would consider the offer. Three weeks later she burst into the gallery. She was "ready for bear." Angry. Shaking. Demanding that my staff person have me, the owner, call her. She yelled the story that a friend even had to tell her that her earring looked as if it was falling off. And it did! And it shouldn't have! And why weren't we taking care of her in a proper way. Like giving her an earring replacement free.

When I arrived at work the woman had left. My staff person was near tears. She had tried to do everything as she had been taught. She quietly listened. She assured the customer she would tell the owner. But she did do one thing. The staff person showed her how secure the back was on the remaining earring. C sneered and said, "Well, yes! This isn't the earring I lost!" There was only one thing that seemed appropriate. Get the customer out of the gallery as quickly as possible. Give her exactly what she wanted. Remove her name from the mailing list. Let her know she was no longer welcome.

And so I did. I wrote the check. I put it in an envelope. I put a stamp on it. I was ready. I called and the minute C answered I said, "I have written you a refund for the entire amount. The check is in the mail." I hung up. She was still talking.

I've never hung up on a customer before. I felt horrible. Except for writing about it at this very moment, I will erase the entire incident from my mind. I will erase her name from the computer.

Done.

Over.

Today was a perfect customer day. Six customers walked in and out of the gallery. Four customers needed directions to the bathrooms. Five jewelry artists came through. Two administrators from a national arts organization visited. Five people came to see the ABeCeDarian show. The sun came out. Two customers purchased. What more could I want?

*A slight disclaimer. These customers are composites. I didn't want anyone to feel left out. I didn't want anyone insulted. I've mixed up their traits, but should they figure out which composite they are, yes, we love you. And no we don't love that last one.

CHAPTER EIGHTEEN
RANT AND RAVE

Customers to rave about, Earl & Charyl Kay Sedlik

Rave: The husband who says, "My wife told me that whatever I buy at Facèré is what she wants." We keep a list of past successful purchases to help direct such husbands to the next successful purchase. Everybody's happy!

Rant: Early on, when we sold antique furniture, a customer eyed a set of pressed-back chairs. My dad had refinished the set. My mom had woven six new cane seats for the set. The customer found one chair marked $125. I had forgotten to write, EACH on that tag. I explained to her that the price was not for the set, but for each chair. The customer demanded I sell her the set, and if I didn't she would talk to her lawyer-husband and he would make me sell her the set. I crumbled.

Rave: A wonderful gentleman has flown twice from Palm Desert to Seattle for the sole purpose of shopping at Facèrè. He buys numerous gifts. Why? Because of a refund. We discovered that his first purchase had been tagged wrong. We mailed a note of apology and a check for $300. He called to say that never in his life had he ever received money back from a retailer. That December he flew up to holiday shop and then in the middle of the summer he flew up again. We love him as much as he loves us.

Rant: Then there is the $13,000 sale that ended up being a $1,300 sale. A rare 1830s necklace and earrings in its original box had lost its tag. When my staff person typed in the price she missed a zero and sold the set for $1300 instead of $13,000. After the customer left, my staff person realized her mistake. She immediately went to the hotel where the out-of-town buyers were staying. It was raining. It was cold. My staff person waited in front of the hotel, tears streaming down her face, and sighed with relief when she saw the mother and daughter approaching the hotel. She stopped them. She told them exactly what had happened. She assumed there would be no problem. The mother took immediate control. And with great consternation said that it wasn't their fault we ran such a poorly managed store. Her exact words, "Mistakes are how you learn, young lady. No I will not return the purchase. It belongs to us."

And the staff person deserves a rave. She insisted, on the threat that she would no longer work for me, that I let her trade her personal jewelry collection to make up the difference. It is five years later and she is still with Facèré, tenure of twenty-five years. She is one of the most wonderful employees one could ever want.

Rave: There are customers who have a piece of jewelry on lay-away at any given moment. They pay off one and purchase another. They come to visit once a month. They pay steadily and with great cheer.

Rant and Rave: One of our very best customers has had a piece on lay-away for over a year. She paid the first and second payments. It has now been ten months and we have not heard from her. We've written notes saying all she needs to do is keep the account alive with the most minimal of payments or let us know she no longer wishes to purchase the piece. Perhaps she is ill. Perhaps she has lost her job. This is a confusing situation. We wrote her a note that we will put the item out for sale if we do not hear from her in one month. She can maintain and use her credit whenever she wishes. We hope she is all right. If she reads this, we hope she will call or e-mail.

Rant: A woman receives a gift from our gallery. She does not like it. She waits three months to return it. She chooses another piece. She leaves happy. She returns two months later. She does not like her choice. She wants money. We say, "No." She can trade. She leaves.

Two weeks later she walks in as if nothing had happened. She trades for a pair of earrings. The difference is $2.75. I give her the change. I think (I hope!) she is happy.

Rave: A couple comes to the gallery to buy wedding bands. They pick up an 1880s band which is inscribed. Inside the band are the initials, B.W. to K. M. 1884. The initials are theirs! Goosebumps all around.

Rant: A customer calls to tell me, "I am one of your best customers. I'd like you to donate to my environmental cause." I tell him that I am on an arts board, and all of my discretionary giving is to that cause. He responds, "If you don't give, and give generously, I'll never shop with you again." I didn't. He didn't.

Rave: Many young jewelers come into the gallery and ask thoughtful, insightful questions. They handle the jewelry with awe and respect. They understand if we have to leave them for a buying customer. They wait patiently and have more great questions. They are a pleasure.

Rant (but then...): I walk into Vanity Fair at Pier 70 to Jim Morgan's greeting, "We've just been shoplifted." I ask, "Are you sure?" "Positively. A Ruby ring." "Describe him." "Short, Eighteen. Male. Red T-shirt."

I grab the Polaroid camera we use for photographing appraisals and I'm out the door. "Wait, maybe you shouldn't..." I hear as I leave and ignore the warning. I yell back, "I'm going to go find him!"

I do! Minutes later I stand in front of a young man in a red shirt.

"What are you doing?" he demands.

"I'm taking your picture."

"Why?"

"I just might need it." I snap the picture and I walk away because it dawns on me I've probably done something really stupid.

Back at the store, I call 911.

The police arrive. Take the photo. Minutes later, one officer returns to announce, "We got him! He said he didn't know what we were talking about, but when we checked his pockets, we found this." The officer holds up a ring. My ring.

"Do you want to press charges or do you want your merchandise back?"

"I want the ring back." Later, I think, what happened to my outrage, my sense of justice? It vanished. I just wanted the ring.

The policeman leaves (with the ring...evidence) and returns with a good story. They told the kid that the woman whose ring he had just wanted it back. No charges. The kid said it was his ring. It was a coincidence. The cops cuffed him, opened the car trunk, and found items from every store on Pier 70.

Weeks passed. I received a notice to be at the kid's hearing. Perhaps I would be called as a witness. Turns out he pleaded guilty that morning, so that when they brought him into the courtroom it was for sentencing.

He entered the room with two guards. Cuffed. In jail pajamas. He looked around the room. His eye caught mine. He lifted his shackled hands and waved. To me. Like we were old friends.

Broke my heart.

And, yes I got the ring back.

Rave: Jordan is a child of five. She has blond hair, cut like the hair of the child on the Dutch cleanser tin. While waiting for her mom to get off work, her dad brought Jordan to visit Facèré.

The first day they stood outside studying jewelry in a window. I heard her dad read the information that accompanies each artist's display. He reduced the words to manageable bites: "This is the work of Alisa Miller. She lives in Chicago. She works in silver and gold."

"Oh!" Jordan's response put a bright exclamation point to the end of her father's sentence. They moved to the next case and he read the next description, "This is the work of Biba Shutz."

"Biba?" Jordan asked, pleased at the double syllables. She laughed a bright, clear cascade and repeated, "Bi-ba-shutz!"

Now they entered the gallery. I acknowledged the dad's informative reading to his daughter with the words, "You can't start too young!"

With pride, he brought her to be introduced, "This is Jordan. She loves jewelry!" I shake her hand. "And I'm Karen. And I love jewelry, too!"

He walked her around the gallery, reading three or four more cards. When they got back to the front desk, he stepped back and directed Jordan, "Tell the lady what lasts forever."

"Well," she said, and honest true, she placed her pointing finger just beside the dimple in her cheek, "What lasts forever are diamonds and..." she paused, as if for effect or perhaps to remember the word, she said, "...and infinity."

Over the weeks we've almost become friends. One Monday she told me that her weekend project with Fimo (having seen the work of Cynthia Toops), didn't go so well. "It broke," was her concluding analysis. "But I'm not giving up."

Then one day, she did what I think a very large percentage of the women in the world do. She headed to the diamond case tugging her father along. She pointed and said, "I like that one. Oh, and look at that one!" Her fingers made round smudges on the case, enthusiastically finding her next favorite diamond.

She is attracted by something deep and unexplainable, something that lasts forever, right there, along with infinity.

Rants and raves? Comes with the territory.

CHAPTER NINETEEN
PAY ATTENTION,
THIS IS YOUR MOTHER SPEAKING!

A gift not to return

In Chapter Thirteen, I touched on the subject of returning gifts. I think the subject deserves its own chapter. I'm repeating myself the tiniest bit, but some subjects need repeating.

Let's reset the scene: A gentleman enters the gallery. He studies the cards that identify each artist's work. He opens and closes the drawers. I can hear him making thoughtful noises with his mouth, "ummm," 'tsk, tsk," "sigh."

"You look like a man on a mission," I say.

"Birthday," he responds and he leans into the display. "She's very classic, but she likes the unusual."

Building A Business, Building A life

We look at numerous pieces and within minutes he's focused on three pairs of earrings.

"But she said no more earrings." He sighs and then says, almost beseechingly, "It probably doesn't matter, she'll just return it."

Before he makes his final choice, he has discarded the earrings, and has had me try on a French antique necklace, an enamel necklace containing star anise, and a chain that can be doubled or worn in a single swath. Two other staff members come over to add their opinions. Sometimes we even vote and we share the reasons for voting for one piece over another.

The customer starts to smile. He assures us, and assures himself that the chain necklace is a perfect choice. He, with a jaunty flourish, hands over his charge card. He loves the gift wrap! We are all smiles.

"I think we've chosen just the right gift!" he says as he leaves. He waves and says, "Thank you for all your attention. I think I nailed it this time!"

We return the dozen items to their display. We think maybe this was the perfect gift. He was so thoughtful. He took his time. He was so happy. He was so pleased with himself.

A week later she walks in and huffily slaps his gift on our counter. "I don't know what he could have been thinking!"

AND NOW THE LECTURE:

Customers are not always right. Especially you women who return your husband's gifts are not right.

You are wrong. Believe me, you are wrong. Listen up! If you are that wife who returns gifts, pay attention. If you disagree with the stated fact that you should not return a gift, let me tell you, you are really, really wrong.

How do I know? I am an authority on gifts returned by wives.

Close your eyes and imagine your husband. Imagine him on your first date. The excitement. The pleasure. He's trying so hard. To be nice. To be intelligent. To be charming.

Now imagine your husband entering my gallery. Imagine him moving from case to case. Hold that image and try, please try, to believe what I am going to say. Suspend all doubt. Let me describe your husband. While he is looking for a gift for you, he is like he was on that first date: trying so hard, trying to win your heart, trying to be his best "nice," trying to choose intelligently, anticipating the moment he will charm you! To win you once again.

He chooses. He purchases. He holds the wrapped gift tenderly, securely.

And that is what you unwrap: his excitement, his thoughtfulness, his charm, his pleasure in pleasing you.

Now, follow my instructions. You are to say, "Thank you" and you are to mean it. You are thanking him for recalling everything the two of you were on your first date.

That is his gift. And don't you dare return it.

POSTSCRIPT
TWELVE TWICE AND THRICE TOLD TALES

Surprise!

"The best stories are the ones you tell over and over and each begins with, Do you remember..." my mom.

1. Yes, But What Is It?

At a staff meeting we passed around the photograph of twelve doughnuts in a wire basket. The photograph was sent by a Korean jewelry artist living in San Francisco and the image was for use in a four-color advertising card for a show entitled NEW MAKERS/ Fresh Visions. The show was a jewelry art show and the doughnuts were supposed to be jewelry.

We each eyed the photograph to determine which doughnut we would make our own. The choice would be difficult. Sprinks? Chocolate? Sugar? Glazed? We could hardly wait until the pieces arrived.

Five weeks later the mailman delivered a package. Each doughnut lay tenderly nestled in tissue. Four rows of four doughnuts. And, five doughnut holes as a bonus. Each doughnut the correct size and shape, but hinged, constructed of copper and enamel.

The staff allowed me the honor of choosing first and I chose chocolate.

Susan asked, "How do you wear it?"

I turned the doughnut over and over. No pin stem. No finding for a necklace. Too large for a ring. Too small for a bracelet. It had a hinge. What was it? No one could figure it out.

I called the artist. She barely spoke English. "What are they?" I asked. The phone crackled over her accent and I thought she said, "Body adornment."

"But how do you wear them?" I said slowly, and stupidly, and I'm sure, loudly.

She repeated, "Body adornment."

Confused, I tried to think of another way to solve the mystery.

Enunciating each word precisely, I answered, "There...is...no...pin...stem."

She giggled. "No, no pin stem."

"It won't fit on my wrist."

"Yes. Not your wrist."

"What are they?"

"For your body."

It was futile. I thanked her and hung up. Not

Building A Business, Building A life

knowing how to wear them, we all lost interest in purchasing. But, what the hey! They were fun and different and interesting. When the show opened, the basket was in the first case, front and center.

Two days into the show, my hair dresser dropped by the gallery.

"This your new show?" he asked and walked around the nine cases displaying the work of nine different artists. He stopped in front of the doughnut display. He looked at me and raised an eyebrow. "My, my, my, Karen, this is most daring of you."

"What?" I asked.

"These rings," he answered.

"Rings?"

"You truly don't know what they are, do you?"

"No. We can't figure out how to wear them."

"Indeed. Well, little missy, here's a bit of news." He put a finger in the air and twirled it as if it might hold a doughnut and he wiggled his finger. "Cock rings," he said. "You're selling cock rings."

The story doesn't end there.

Susan, the staff person in charge of news releases, had sent a personal letter and the advertising card to the president of Krispy Kreme. We thought he might be enticed to see the show and purchase a doughnut. Thank goodness, he was not enticed.

The story continued.

A Bellevue matron walked through the gallery. "What are these?" she asked, leaning over the case,

eyeing the doughnut with pink frosting.
"You don't want to know," I answered.
"Of course I want to know."
"No, not really."
"Don't condescend to me, young lady."
So I told her.
She's never been back.

And the last episode:
We got a call from New York. A gentleman asked, "About the doughnuts. Do you have the chocolate one and the one with sprinks?"
I didn't tell him we had not sold any. "Yes, we still do!"
"I'd like to buy those two, please."
After he hung up we had a staff conference.
"What if he doesn't know?" Dana asked.
"What if he returns them after the show is over?" Susan wondered.
"And we've already sent the work back and then we're stuck with them," Helen added.
"What shall we do?" Lorraine mused.
I'm the boss. I called the customer.
"Hello, this is Karen from Facèré Jewelry Art Gallery in Seattle. About the doughnuts…"
"I know what they are."
And that was that!

2. No Rain for Red Umbrellas

There's nothing like a parade. I opened a second downtown location with the toot and blare of a New

Building A Business, Building A life

Orleans four-piece brass band. Dozens of red balloons. Dozens of red umbrellas. A red ribbon across the door. Red Vines. Rosé wine. Customers in black-tie and tennis shoes. Each person received a gift of a red umbrella and with the umbrellas twirling over our heads we gathered at the Facèré Jewelry Salon at the Sheraton Hotel and followed the Dixieland band as it tooted us from the hotel to the second location. Thirty or so customers danced through the hotel lobby, down the steps, across Sixth Avenue, down Pike, across Fifth, one more block down Pike, across Fourth, took a turn and entered the cavernous lobby of Century Square. The blare and blast of the trumpets bounced off the curved-arch ceiling.

Along the way people had cheered, parted to let us pass, danced a few old-soft-shoe steps with us.

It was only after Terry Axelrod, president of the President's Club of the Chamber of Commerce had cut the ribbon on the new store, did she ask a crucial question: "Karen, how did you ever get a parade permit?"

Parade permit?
Hadn't crossed my mind.

3. A Little Bit of L.A.

A gentleman came into the Sheraton Facèré Jewelry Salon. He had a certain aura about him: a slight swagger in the hips, slicked-back hair, yellow-silk shirt, wine-colored pleated pants, no socks. Self-assured. As I watched him browse, I tried to put a name to him. Who was he? The way he worked around the edge of the shop made me think I'd seen this guy before. So familiar. But no name came to mind. He browsed. He left. That afternoon I went next door to the Sheraton Sundries Store to buy a newspaper and the mystery was solved. *Vanity Fair Magazine.* On the cover. The very man. And I realized why I hadn't recognized him. My memory was of flowing hair, a jaunty Australian outback hat, a wild, drugged expression. He'd changed. He was no longer the Easy Rider. He was the new Dennis Hopper.

Another Hollywood story...
You can tell when the movie crews are in town. They wear jackets, the back of which are heavily embroidered with their production logo. A guy came in. He answered my greeting and comments with "Huh?" "Yeah" and "Um, okay." Each response a breath-releasing thud. "May I show you something?" "Nah." "You must be with the production company for *Rocky Three*." "Got it."

He left.

An observant customer commented, "Must be Stalone's speech coach."

And...

Kris Kristofferson walked through the hotel lobby. It is apparent that when they film him, they must shoot from the knees up. He has such presence in films. Such power. He appears on screen as a big man.

Nope.

Kris Kristofferson is short.

4. Placing First

Display work rotated between staff members. Who could out-do whom? Jim's tour-de-force was created with game boards: Chutes and Ladders, Monopoly, Checkers, Chess, Chinese Checkers, Backgammon. Each board filled a single display case and on each board the mover was a piece of jewelry. Lael created historical figures from black and white images and stood them on foam board: Henry VIII, Mark Twain, Queen Victoria, Nicholas and Alexandra, Marie Antoinette. On the bosom of each glowed an antique brooch or a diamond-set stickpin. Not to be outdone, I bought six fish bowls and six angelfish and six slender pieces of seaweed and one package of turquoise rocks. At the bottom of each bowl, in the sand, under the water, I stuck a gold brooch. Success was mine! Except when I handed a dripping pin to a professional woman wearing a silk blouse and she pressed it to the collar of her suit. A drip. A stain. A cleaning bill.

Probably not the best display.
But pretty!

Very soon, to six different customers, we gave away each fish in its bowl. One customer tried to say "no thank-you" but his tow-headed five-year-old son insisted he had wanted a fish his whole life! The father relented and the father came back to tell us our little gift had cost him six hundred dollars. He had to purchase a tank, a filter, and another fish. It wasn't the six hundred dollars that had been the biggest problem. It was his son watching the angelfish consume each fish as a companion was slid into the water.

Who knew?

Angelfish are not communal. Right! Otherwise known as Angel Sharks!

5. Knowing Your Customer

Vanity Fair, my second location on the second floor of Pier 70, glowed with light: highly polished hardwood floors, soft-white globes from an old school house, mirrored images from Plexiglas cases, filtered light through three six-foot stained-glass windows, all enhanced by the dancing light off of Puget Sound. The antique merchandise was a perfect fit to this tucked-away space: first edition books, silver serving pieces, porcelain figures, Early American Sandwich glass, Limoges china, Majolica dinnerware, Belleek ware—everything rare and choice.

When I remember it now, it surprises me that anyone ever found us on the second floor of the northern most pier on Seattle's waterfront. Word of mouth kept this tiny, exquisite shop in business.

On a memorable day, when I was alone at the counter, two men walked in. They didn't just walk in, they descended. Well dressed. Well coiffed. Inquisitive. There wasn't anything they didn't want to see. The number of items on the counter grew: a sterling napkin ring, a leather-bound edition of *Leaves of Grass*, sugar tongs, a Georgian fish slice.

Should they buy everything, it would be the largest sale, ever! All I could think of was please, oh

Building A Business, Building A life

please, don't ask to write a check.

"Think we've about done it," one said.

"May we write a check?" the other added.

They had been so friendly, so enthusiastic, it was all I could do to call up the courage to say, "Yes, but I need to see a picture ID."

"No problem," the shorter, rounder one answered.

He took out his wallet. It unfolded, each section falling open like he was playing a deck of magical cards. On each was his name:

Robert Joffrey
        Robert Joffrey
                Robert Joffrey.

Robert Joffrey of the Robert Joffrey Ballet.

So ended a day to remember. Always.

6. Being Really Mean

My first location, North Country Fair, held a hundred testaments to the early 1900s: copper kettles, a kitchen queen, a curved tin-top trunk, a wall of farmer's tools—rakes and hoes and a shovel and a grain sifter—across from which stood a barrel of shoe-lasts and wooden planes. The warm brown woods, oiled and smelling of linseed, played against generous bouquets of paper zinnias in prismatic colors of ruby, goldenrod, sunflower yellow, and flamingo pink.

One day, a man in professional attire entered the shop, maneuvered his way through the collection of stuff until he stood next to the barrel. He reached for a twelve-inch wooden plane, held it in his arms and caressed it as if it were already his.

"Greetings," I called. "Lovely, isn't it?"

"What's your best price?" Before I could answer he continued, "I'll give you ten bucks for it. Isn't worth more than that. I know. I collect tools."

It wasn't unusual for someone to ask for a discount. In fact I often discounted. I discounted if someone was pleasant. I discounted if someone was demanding. I discounted and never considered the consequences (like, was I making any money?).

He inspected the blade. He scrutinized the shape and the size and the weight of the plane. He was waiting me out.

From where I stood, I saw the price tag: twenty-seven dollars. How could he not possibly see it was worth every penny? In fact, the plane was worth more than it was marked. Which prompted me to do one of the meanest things I have ever done.

"Take it," I said.

"Oh, no, I can't do that."

"Sure, take it." And what came to mind was the Bible verse, "Heaping coals of fire on your enemies head." I'm not even sure that's what that Bible verse means, but it seemed like that's what I was doing. Being more than nice! Being nice until coals of fire were heaped, and heaped, and heaped on his head.

"It's yours," I insisted. "You don't have to pay anything for it."

"No, I can't do that," he said, bewildered.

"You can. You need it."

I came out from behind the counter with a store sack in my hand. I reached for the plane and jammed it in the sack. I handed the package to him and I opened the door.

"Goodbye. It's been my pleasure."

"But…"

I closed the door.

He might have been stupid and pushy, but I was mean. I was not proud of myself. I vowed never to be placed in that situation again. I decided then and there, no more discounting. Ever.

7. If You Don't Succeed…

We keep a Want Box—customers' requests for items not in stock. The want box is a 3x5 file, twenty-four inches long. The box is filled with cards requesting love tokens, animal parts, three-carat diamonds, enamels, miniatures, fox images and dragonfly images and bull images, muff chains and platinum chains and chains made of hair, coffin shapes, sewing utensils, car images, plane images, anything and everything that collectors collect.

When we call someone whose name is in the Want Box, we make a point of saying, "You requested we call." If we don't say "you requested," the person thinks we are cold-calling and they hang up. Fortunately for us, the customer usually says something like, "I can't believe you still have my name." And if it is a serious collector, he or she says, 'I'll be right down! Don't sell it!'

Jim Morgan was working the Want Box. He dialed the wrong number.

"Is this Margaret Lewis?"

"No, you must have the wrong number."

"This isn't the person who requested we call if we got in a Victorian tiger-claw brooch?"

"No, there is no one here who would want anything like that!"

Undaunted, Jim continued, "You know, it's so rare and wonderful, you just might want to see it!"

She didn't.

Jim hung up and Lael and I burst into laughter.

Such great audacity. Such great enthusiasm. Such conviction. Who wouldn't want a Victorian tiger-claw brooch?

8. Breath Taking

I was deep into a ledger of numbers finishing the previous day's books.

A shuffle.

A movement.

A raggedy man crawled through the door.

My heart stopped. My hand shook so violently I could barely punch in 911.

The man crawled and turned behind a case.

I yelled into the receiver, "There's a man crawling into my shop!"

With practiced calm, the operator said, "Are you in danger?"

That helped. The crawler seemed totally oblivious to me. He wasn't aware I had called the police. He kept crawling. I could see his bare feet between the cases.

"Please send someone," I whispered.

"Someone is on the way."

Within minutes two policemen came through the door, hoisted the man up by his armpits and took him outside.

One policeman returned to make a report.

"Are you okay?" he asked.

"Just a bit shaken."

He took the report, though there wasn't much to say.

"What's wrong with him?" I asked.

"Not much. I hate to tell you this, but he might have thought your space was a bathroom. It's small, it's accessible. And at the moment he is peeing on the parking meter."

9. Before Sleepless In Seattle

"Is that a street person?" I wrote on a scrap of paper as Kim and I stood at the counter at the City Centre Facèré Jewelry Art Gallery.

Kim took the pen from my hand and wrote, "No, that's Meg Ryan."

"Who's Meg Ryan?" I wrote back.

Kim looked at me as if I were crazy. "I'll take care of this customer."

And she did.

Just shows-to-go-you, that out of context even someone as beautiful as Meg Ryan can shop without being recognized.

At least by one person.

10. Gift Giving

Another Robert Joffrey tale. Over the years, Robert shopped with us for thank-you gifts for his Seattle hostess. In the Sheraton Hotel Facèré Salon, on the counter, were three samples of our gift wrap—each with a decorative tie-on: a bumble bee, a flower, and a metal heart. Mr. Joffrey chose the bumble-bee. We wrapped the gift and put through his charge. We tissue-wrapped the package and put the gift in a Facèré sack. He bid us goodbye and promised to see us next trip.

I straightened the counter.

As I reached to put the third sample gift wrap box back in place, I realized it wasn't empty! Which meant Robert Joffrey's hostess would be opening a beautifully gift-wrapped empty box.

In a panic, we called the number on his check: Robert Joffrey Ballet Company, New York.

In a rush of words I said, "Help! I'm calling from Seattle. I need to know where Robert is staying!"

"Robert?"

"Mr. Joffrey."

"That is privileged information."

In the most pleading voice, I replayed the sale, step by step. "He's going to present that gift and she's going to open an empty box!"

The other end of the line found the story wonderfully amusing and divulged the information that Mr. Joffrey was registered at the Sorrento.

I thanked and thanked her.

We called a cab. We told the cabby that someone had to sign for the package and he needed to call us to tell us it had arrived.

We didn't relax until Robert Joffrey called. He thought it was a hoot and he even offered to return the empty box. We told him we thought we could find another.

11. Now You See It, Now You Don't

Another delivery was truly catastrophic. To Kurt Cobain we sold Courtney Love's engagement ring. The ring was an Edwardian masterpiece of twining leaves, fluid flowers, millegrained edges, pierced surfaces—all in delicately worked platinum holding a dozen brilliant, but small, diamonds.

Courtney soon returned with a problem. She told us with dramatic gesture and demanding words, she needed something more! She was about to film her first major video. She needed something, for God's sake, that showed! Something big. Something glittery. Something her audience wouldn't miss!

She left the ring and we had our bench jeweler create a diamond "jacket" which surrounded the original ring. Six diamonds to a side. Absolutely seeable!

The ring finished, we called Courtney. She was in New York. We offered to mail the ring.

No, no, she'd have her "runner" pick it up.
As he left, I called, "Be sure to insure it!"
He didn't.

The last time the ring was seen was at the front desk of Courtney's New York hotel. The ring never made it to her room.

There isn't a photograph of Courtney Love that I don't look at her left hand. With sadness.

12. The Wild Nigerian Foot Massager

I was alone at Vanity Fair on the second floor of Pier 70. A young man with what sounded like a Haitian accent, greeted me with a smile and a lilting, "How ya doin?" He walked up one side of the shop and down the other. He stopped at the end of the counter.

Looking down at my feet, as if he had discovered a hidden treasure, he exclaimed, "What interesting shoes you have!"

I looked down at my clogs and wondered what he could be talking about.

"Can I see how they are made?"

He leaned over as if he might grab my shoe, and to thwart him, I reached down, took off the shoe, and handed it to him.

"That is an amazing piece of work," he said and he studied the shoe as if it were very, very rare.

Then he kneeled and held out his hand for my foot. Instead of pushing the shoe on, an easy slip, he began massaging my foot.

I was horrified. "Please! Don't do that." And at that very moment made up the sentence, "I can't stand someone touching my feet!"

I must have kind-of yelled, because he backed away, "No problem. Just thought you've been on your feet all day and a nice massage is what most people would enjoy!"

"Well, I'm not most people." I flipped pages of

my ledger to show how busy I was and I started making decisive entries in hopes that he would go away.

He got the message and left.

The minute he was out the door, I called downstairs to my friend, Vincent, who owned Getchell Hill Boots, a shoe store.

In a challenging, smug voice, I said, "Hi, Vinnie. I'll bet your customers don't massage your feet."

"What?"

"This guy was just here and he tried to massage my foot."

"IT'S THE WILD NIGERIAN FOOT MASSAGER. CALL THE POLICE!"

"Are you serious?" I said, not understanding in any way why he was yelling at me.

"OF COURSE I'M SERIOUS! YESTERDAY'S PAPER! CALL THE POLICE."

I dialed 911. "This isn't an emergency. I just want to report a strange incident. This man was just in my shop. He tried to massage my foot."

"We'll send someone over."

I waited and within the hour in walked a policeman and a policewoman.

My first words were, "Don't you dare laugh!"

Of course, they laughed. Then they took the report.

The next day a second article appeared in *The Seattle Times*: "Woman Felled by Shoe Thief. A man accosted a woman on Fifth Avenue. He pushed her to the ground and ran away with her shoe. Bystanders chased the man and held him until the police arrived.

He was arrested and charged with assault. An investigation of his living premises revealed over one hundred single shoes."

The Wild Nigerian Foot Massager was no longer out there offering massages.

So ends twelve of the best stories from the past thirty-seven years.

After forty years in business, I have experienced all types of customers and interesting situations. I still love my business. I love my customers. I love jewelry art and its makers. My staff is wonderful.

To all of my customers, artists, browsers, friends, acquaintances, strangers, or whoever you are reading this book, I hope your box is always full and thank-you for the abundance of memories.

WORKBOOK CHAPTER ONE
IN THE BEGINNING

How to start

You have a business dream. You have some business knowledge—you more than likely had a lemonade stand at age five, a retail summer job in high school, you waitressed in college, babysat forever, and you've shopped your whole life.

That's how much business experience I had. If I can do it, you can do it.

To start your business, make a list of the people you know, what you need, and what you want.

Who you know (be specific, list by name)

- Parents
- Spouse/partner
- Friends who will become customers
- A lawyer
- An accountant
- A bookkeeper (for years I did my own bookkeeping, but when I was finally able to hire a bookkeeper, it was heaven!)
- Anyone you know who owns a small business

- Anyone you know who has a large business
- The one friend you have that shops the most (All of the above are eligible for your first focus group)
- Acquaintances of any kind (pick up cards at your cleaners, the restaurants you frequent, your dentist, all the places you shop, anyone and everyone)

With this list, begin your mailing list for hard copy and for email.

What you need

- A book that inspires! If you can find *Minding the Store* by Stanley Marcus of Neiman/Marcus, you will have a winner. If not that book, look for other first person accounts of people who have created a business. You'll need inspiration along the way. Choose books about businesses larger than you imagine you'll ever be.
- Books with down-to-earth details on businesses of the size you imagine...there are a slew of these books. Buy one; be sure it has a sample business plan. When you've finished mining this first "how-to" book, choose one other that is different in style and determination. That's it. Two books to begin with are plenty, otherwise you will end up with a bunch of books that say the same thing over and over and you'll be reading too much and acting too little.
- A budget (double every expense and include a salary from the first day).
- An outline of a business plan, with plenty of white space to be filled in as you proceed.

What You Want

- Money. Check your savings. Consider what you might borrow from a member of your family. If you should borrow from a family member, create a contract with a payment schedule. Include the interest you will pay—even if you should borrow from your wonderful, indulgent mother or from your uncle who has money stashed in his floor joists, you still need a contract.
- A business plan. Adapt the business plan for your business dream from the first book you bought – no more than five pages that you will change regularly, so not to worry if the plan isn't complete or perfect.
- A space. Look at every For Lease sign you pass by immediately thinking: will the space behind this sign work for me? Is it safe? Is there easy access? Is there parking? Is it large enough? Is there storage? What kind of people walk by this space? Continue to add questions to this list and don't worry about going inside to see the real space.
- When you are ready to see your banker, take along your accountant. Two of you will look more impressive than one, and when the banker asks you a difficult question, you might need another voice, if not some breathing space.

An Advisory Group

- Go through the above lists and choose six to eight acquaintances
- Write a formal letter (a real letter!) explaining what you are doing—the name of your business, your possible

location, your merchandise mix.
- In the letter explain why you have written them (you admire them, he or she is a close friend, they have business acumen, etc).
- Explain that you will call in a couple of days to confirm attendance and answer any questions they might have. (Do not include in this group professionals you might later hire, such as a lawyer or an accountant. You need to pay those professionals.)
- Be sure to tell each person about the other people you have invited so that they know they will be with a group of intelligent, interesting people (another reason they will want to join you).
- Serve the best cookies and the best coffee.
- Keep the meeting to exactly two hours no matter how good the conversation.
- Later you might choose all or some of this group to meet with you once a quarter.
- At your second meeting show an action plan that grew from the first evening's discussion.
- List at least ten action items to be accomplished in the first month to move you from dreaming to actual goals.
- Show them a calendar on which you circle, in red, the date you want your business to open.
- Tell your group that you will need at least six months to get off the ground and then you would like to meet with them at least two more times, six months apart to see how well you are doing.
- On your first anniversary, invite everyone on your mailing list to a celebration and publicly acknowledge your Advisory Board.

You have work to do

Time to start.

WORKBOOK CHAPTER TWO
BABY STEPS, BIG STEPS

What I did wrong...no need for you to make similar mistakes

Don't choose a location without verifying (in writing!) that the space is commercially zoned.

Don't choose a location that has twenty-five steps to the front door. Why?

- Half of all of your customers can't climb twenty-five steps.
- You have no visible front window to display your merchandise.
- You'll have to invest in large signs to let customers know who you are, what you do, and what you have, and they still won't climb twenty-five steps.

Don't think pricing is magic. Know your pricing before you begin. Buy price guides, go online, and go shopping at your competitors. Don't guess at prices!

Don't depend solely on your parents. My folks were great, but they were also generous beyond most parents' point of endurance.

Don't treat those who make you a loan less than you would treat a bank. Be clear: You've accepted a loan. Keep business relationships business-like, e.g. have contracts, written agreements, pay schedules, and you pay interest.

When you are ready to approach a bank, you need to have a business plan which includes the following:

- Cover letter to the person with whom you've made an appointment
- History/executive summary
- Definition of your business
- Definition of your market
- Product description
- Objectives and goals
- A five-year budget (best and worst case scenarios)
- Location/improvements
- Personal resume/bio/financial position

Once you are open, don't fool yourself about the money you are making. Have a budget and check that budget daily!

What I did right…and what you might consider doing

Invite all your friends to your business opening and to all other events your business offers, for example: readings, guest appearances, trunk shows, traveling shows, curated displays.

Include in your invitations your siblings, your grocer, your teachers, past friends, and all of your lost relatives.

Have a selection of merchandise for a variety of tastes and a variety of pocket books.

Don't underestimate being pleasant and enthusiastic when speaking to possible landlords (and remember, they might need you more than you need them!).

Be sure your sources for merchandise can replenish what you sell in a timely manner.

Now, it's your turn

With paper and pencil in hand, visit at least three of your favorite retail locations. Be generous with your observations. Observe and write more than you think you need to remember.

1. Does the signage let you know what's inside? Does it make you want to go inside? Is the entrance clean and inviting?

2. What is in the windows? Are the windows cluttered? Fun? Simple? Elegant? What about the display tells the store's story?

3. Is the door open? Did you have to be buzzed in? Is there an off-duty policeman at the door?

Building A Business, Building A life

4. What kind of shoppers are coming and going? What are their ages? Try to determine what made them enter the store. What made them leave?

5. How were customers greeted? How did they answer? What was the physical distance between the clerk and the customer? Did the clerk make eye contact? Did the clerk come from behind the counter to greet the customer?

6. How many people entered while you were there? Of those, how many purchased? How long did individuals stay in the shop? (The longer a customer stays in a retail location, the more likely they will buy.)

7. How safe is this location? Check the neighborhood. Will this location be vulnerable to shoplifting? Armed robbery? Break-in?

8. Once inside the front door, what is directly to your right? (Most shoppers immediately look to the right. That first display is their first impression.) Start thinking about your dream location. What will you put to the right?

9. How do the customers move through the shop? Is there a path? Is merchandise easily visible? Touchable? (And if it is touchable, what precautions are there against shop-lifting?)

10. Determine what bathroom facilities are available for

your staff and for your customers.

11. Determine the distance to the nearest bank.
(You need easy access at least once a day...how far will you have to walk to make a deposit?)

12. What did you like most about this shop? What can you repeat in your location? What made you feel welcome? Interested? What might make you buy?

13. Give each shop a grade (F to A+)...grade quickly. Now think why.

The staff and I think of Facèrè Jewelry Art Gallery as "our living room." It is a place where we spend a good part of each day and we love being there. What will make you comfortable, proud, excited, and at home in your space?

Now, it is time to make your dream come true! Good luck!

WORKBOOK CHAPTER THREE
THIS WASN'T IN ANY BUSINESS PLAN

What to learn?

Sometimes life comes along and whops you up-side-the-head. It is forty-some years later, and I still don't know how a person prepares for the big events in his or her life. The big events? One of the biggest events in my life was divorce. And strangely enough, I think having someone steal something from the gallery is also a "big event."

The rules are broken. I lose faith. I don't know how to trust. Slowly, slowly life shifts and then slowly, slowly life refocuses.

And what has this to do with business?

The divorce moved me into survival mode. Thefts move me into distrust mode. You can organize and fight for survival. Distrust has to wear away. The divorce made me realize I was on my own. My business wasn't half of the income. It was all of the income. I had to learn to run the business as if my life depended on it. It did.

My business became a blessing

I had to open the doors at 9:30. I had to pay the rent. I had to act as if I was strong and happy. I had to answer correspondence, stock new merchandise, greet customers, pay taxes—all of those things that made the business survive. And at least for nine hours a day I knew who I was. For nine hours a day my life had structure, troubles, successes, and goals.

Surprise! I was not alone

After a few weeks of seclusion and self-pity, I attended a lecture for "singles." I could barely believe that an entire room was full of people sharing the facts that they were not sleeping well, they were not eating well, they felt like everyone knew they were single, they felt like they would be sad for the rest of their lives. And, these experiences were so universal that someone could lecture about it. Truly amazing!

The next day after admitting I was truly "single," work was better and I began to tolerate the hours after work.

Friends became very, very important

Friends made me laugh, kept me sane. I searched them out and held them dear.

Creating a second life

I became very busy when I was single I finished a second degree in painting at the University of Washington. I joined Mountaineers. I joined Great Books. I purchased season tickets to the opera, to Act Theatre, and to The Bathhouse Theater. I learned to be single.

For those of you in the midst of the divorce mess, here's an amazing thought: I learned to love being single. I became self-reliant. I kept adding to my life away from the store. The best thing I did? I took Greek dancing lessons (because Greek dancing doesn't require a partner). That's where, after three years of single-hood I met Don. Miracles happen. I could have continued being a satisfied, fulfilled single person. But life had its way, and now some thirty years later, I wear a wedding ring that I swore as a single woman I would never, ever wear again.

Solid advice, hire the "best"

Hire the best divorce attorney. The "best" encourages you to settle with your ex, as much as you can on your own. The "best" is not interested in going to court. The "best" maybe isn't the biggest gun in town, but maybe works for the biggest gun in town. I hired Wolfgang Anderson, now a noted, important divorce attorney.

But then, he was just beginning his practice and after my ex and I settled as much as we could and signed the papers, Wolf charged me $150. The divorce was painful, but at least it was cheap. And that was good for business.

Start a new life

Immediately.

WORKBOOK CHAPTER FOUR
MOVING ON

Blink! Making Critical Decisions

Before you proceed with this workbook chapter, if you haven't already, get yourself to your nearest bookstore and buy *Blink* by Malcolm Gladwell. His writing will get you thinking about making decisions. Sometimes you need to make major decisions in the "blink of an eye."

I made such a decision the day I sold that cast-iron stove. I instinctively knew I wanted to sell something small, unusual, antique, and preferably something that would fit in the palm of my hand. Jewelry! Eureka! And if I chose well, a single piece of jewelry could sell for the same price as a cast-iron stove. Or, if I was smart, lucky, and informed, even more.

With this decision, I also changed from being a generalist to being a specialist. I had a basic knowledge of antique merchandise, but I wanted, within my lifetime, to be an authority. By eliminating china, cut glass, paintings, prints, silver, linens, toys, porcelains, etc., I could focus on one area of the antique world: antique jewelry. And, so I did.

And, with that idea in mind, what might you do?

Find a mentor (or mentors). Mentors don't happen. You need to be out and about, and when someone comes along who knows what you need to know, hire such a person or befriend such a person, or write such a person (really write a letter, not an email, or be so bold as to pick up the phone and call). A mentor needs to be a part of your life. Respect that person's time.

"Respect" might mean monetary compensation. Some people, like your Dad's best friend who has owned a small business for thirty years, might turn down an offer of money, but would gladly go to coffee with you. But you're a professional. You're approaching a professional for help. That person's time is valuable. Offer to pay.

Build a Library

Immediately begin to build your library. You will need it for research, for business ideas, for inspiration, for knowledge.

My library presently numbers about 300 jewelry books, industry magazines, business books, and historical references, catalogues. The library could easily be twice that size, but I have no room (those of you who have seen our back room, know it's overflowing, and those of you who know I live on a houseboat know there are rules: One box of books comes in? One box of books goes out. Weight is a flotation problem and having the biggest library isn't the goal. Having a working library is).

Study those books. Train your eye! Determine what you like, what you might wear, what your customers might wear, and what artists might choose you as their gallery. If you are thinking of a gallery with a variety of art forms, ask the same questions: what might you have in your home or in your office and what artists might wish to show in your gallery.

Then:
- Attend every symposium
- Attend every lecture
- Attend every retail showing
- Visit every possible competitor
- Join your local art museum(s)
- Attend the graduation show of art majors in any University, College, or Art School in your area
- Attend the SNAG (Society of North American Goldsmiths) yearly conference

For years, Mary Lee Hu, the retired head of the jewelry department at the University of Washington and a great mentor, insisted I attend the SNAG conference. At the time I religiously attended an east coast antique jewelry conference and thought that was the limit to my budget. I was wrong. I only wish I had attended SNAG earlier. It's been eighteen years now of attending SNAG conferences. It's where I see what has happened (historical lectures) and what is happening (lectures by the major players in the world of jewelry art), and what will be happening (Portfolio Reviews of student's work). Bedsides learning, getting away from the demands of business is as important as being immersed in the day-to-day managing of a gallery.

Public Speaking - An Integral Part of Learning

As your knowledge grows, as more customers find your business, the day will come when you will be asked to speak. Be prepared.

Check out your local Toastmasters. It is one of the least expensive, best ways to train for public speaking. You think you'll die if you have to give public speeches? You think you'll throw-up? Well, you might. You'll get over it. The day will come when that delicious fear will make you feel pleased, and excited, and important. Public speaking is part of being in business.

Decisions Have Consequences

Deciding to change from general antiques to antique jewelry, in effect eliminated the involvement of my parents. I would guess that most businesses have parental or spousal or sibling involvement. Even for a little time. My parent's involvement was over a number of years. It was Dad's "retirement." My shop was my mother's biggest hobby. When I no longer needed them for my business, it was a sad parting.

Here's what I wish: I wish I'd said thank-you more often. I wish I'd sent them a gift certificate for a dinner out to a restaurant where they would never have treated themselves. I wish I'd made a scrapbook of photos of all the pieces they refinished. I wish I'd kept a diary of all the amazing things they found.

If you want to be a better business person than I ever was, say thank-you, often and in a variety of ways, to parents, to siblings, to your spouse or partner, and to all of your helpful friends.

A Final Consideration

Here's a bit of business advice that is most important: if you have a monetary relationship with any of the people mentioned above, pay back any loan you have taken on time. Pay every month.

It happened that the loan from my parents was business-like. It's now, years later, that I want to say thank-you, again. And I wish they were still here to read this to let them know how important they were.

That's *the* business lesson. Say thank-you. Often.

WORKBOOK CHAPTER FIVE
SOME SURVIVAL SKILLS FOR THE SINGLE WOMAN

Being safe

This workbook chapter is all about safety, and only a few suggestions about what happens if you are "stalked."

1. Be smart (smarter than I was) about the people you date or the people you share your business information with. Now that there is access to criminal checks and credit checks, use the internet.

2. Having two people when you close is not only important, but a safety precaution. You need one person to lock the door, and one person to be aware. On those rare occasions when you open or close the store by yourself, be extra aware, extra cautious.

3. Someone comes into your store/gallery and that person makes you nervous? Trust your instincts. In the worst of situations one of my staff (alone because the second person made a bathroom run) said to such a customer, "I'd love to show you the jewelry, but I've lost my keys (she hadn't)." Another time (we came to believe that the suspicious person waited until there was only one person in the shop) she said, "My partner will

be back in just a minute. We aren't allowed to show jewelry unless there are two of us. Oh. And here she comes!" Another time a kid in a hoodie and pants near falling off, sauntered in and asked if we had gold. We said we didn't. He left. I called Security to make a report. Turned out they were already tracking him on the monitor.

4. There are times when we know we have been "cased." How do we know? Part instinct. Part the way the "caser" moves too quickly from case to case, the way two or three guys show up one after the other (sorry for the sexist observation, but either women are more discreet or we've never had the pleasure of "caserettes"). After which we always call security and make a report.

5. We keep a phone log every day. If we have unusually "interesting" customers about which we are concerned, we write a description in the phone log. Which reminds me of the time a "suspicious" female customer asked to see the most expensive diamond. Her words. We didn't show the ring to her. Those darn keys got lost again.

6. Strange, hang-up phone calls? We note the calls in our phone log. Since the person who stalked me is dead, we have fewer of those calls. If you are ever in a situation when you need to report someone who is harassing you, the personal record you have kept will be an important record for the police. Without a detailed record showing a continued and sustained problem, the police, more likely than not, will have other crimes to

investigate that they perceive are more important than yours.

7. After I had served the restraining order, I never hesitated to call 911. When I saw the stalker anywhere near my gallery, I would call 911. I'd say, "This isn't an emergency, but I want to report that a restraining order that I filed is being violated." Then I would give them my name, address, and answer their questions. Often a policeman would show up within the half hour. However, by then the stalker was usually gone. After I served the restraining order, the police always responded.

Check the stalking and harassment laws in your area. Don't be surprised if it still is the case that unless the person giving you grief does something 'criminal' there isn't much the police can or will do.

8. Occasionally there are people who are a nuisance. When we have someone in or near our gallery who makes us uneasy (yelling, begging, sleeping, loitering) we call our security office and ask them to send an officer.

We explain the seriousness of the situation and ask the officer to:
- Make your presence known, or
- Come into the shop, or
- Send two officers (if we feel <u>any</u> danger)

And once again, in our phone log we write a description of the person: clothing, approximate age, height, weight, identifying characteristics, date and time he/she appeared.

Building A Business, Building A life

9. There is a myth that is often repeated that "street people" are benign. Possibly so. But possibly not. Our security person gently escorts such persons out of our building.

When I am uneasy, after forty years, I trust my unease. I err on the side of caution.

10. During store hours we have two employees in our gallery. It took some time for me to be totally convinced that two people were necessary (which is what every guide book on running a jewelry business states!), mostly because I didn't think I could afford the increased cost. Truth? I can't afford not to. No question, more employee hours cost more. That cost is worth it.

11. As a retail person you must be patient and charming, wary and smart. All at the same time.

12. Here's something I do, and I'm not even sure why I do it, but the minute I feel uneasy, I check the person's shoes. Maybe I'm just storing all the details I'll need for a report, but there's something about shoes that tells you about the person.

13. We have an emergency button that goes directly to the Seattle Police Department. In forty years we have used it once. The police came with guns drawn. My employee ended up being chastised by the police. They told her to never use the button unless she was physically threatened. In this case it was a shoplift of a $3000 diamond ring. The guy grabbed the ring and ran.

Building A Business, Building A life

He didn't have a gun. He didn't threaten her. She was never, ever to use the emergency alarm for a simple heist. No matter how much the merchandise was worth.

14. Make eye contact with every person who enters your retail establishment. Even though you won't remember everyone, if the person is out to do you harm, that person will think you are going to remember him/her.

15. Something to remember:

Being "cased" seems to follow a pattern:
- The person checks out cases quickly
- The person only "studies" the case with diamonds or gold
- The person asks stupid questions (mentioned before, "Got any gold?" or "Is this gold?")
- The person does not like to "chat" or will not make eye contact.

And? I am sorry to say, all of the above is not true if you are cased by a "pro." In that case you'll probably get hit (slight of hand), or have a group invasion and the thieves will come and go before you have a chance to do anything. Obviously, call the police _and_ notify the building security. (An aside: I am often asked why I have an "up-town" location. Why am I not in the "art district"? Why don't I find a less expensive storefront? Security is one of the reasons. Yes, I pay more rent. In exchange, I get such extras as security.)

16. Be wary of the person who walks in with something to sell and begins with the words, "This was my grandmother's." I know that sounds weird to be suspicious, but every time someone uses that sentence, alarms in my brain go off!

17. The gun. Yes, as I said in the "Surviving a Stalker" chapter I did buy a gun. Numerous retailers that I know also have purchased guns. One person I know has a gun on him at all times.

Whether or not you have a gun, I do not have advice. When I purchased my one and only gun, it was a decision made after I felt that I had no other way to protect myself and that I thought the stalker would cause me physical harm.

The police had told me not to buy a gun. I don't remember being given a pamphlet or a written list of reasons why I shouldn't buy a gun. Perhaps that would have stopped me.

But I admit: I was afraid; I felt as if the police couldn't protect me; I lived alone. I bought a gun. A stupid gun. But it was a gun.

Stay well. Stay safe.

Be smart.

WORKBOOK CHAPTER SIX
WHEN THE RIGHT ONE COMES ALONG:
MONEY AND MARRIAGE

Another "Blink" Moment

The "blink" moment was the moment I decided to marry Don. I knew him five weeks. Saying "yes" felt absolutely right. It was right. Thirty-plus years later, it still feels right.

Money Matters

By the time I met and married Don, my ideas about my business were fairly solid. First, it was <u>my</u> business. We didn't have a prenuptial agreement, but we did have a financial agreement.

The following worked for me, and I recommend it for anyone entering into an arrangement where finances might be construed as mixed:

Keep your finances separate. Have your own checking accounts (one for private matters, one for business matters, one joint account). For the first three or four years we even kept a receipt jar in which we threw receipts for cash purchases either one of us made. At the end of the week, we divided up the expenses. Sometimes, if he was bringing in more money or if I was bringing in more money, we shifted who paid what percentage. Over thirty years, we still have those three accounts, but we don't keep the receipt jar. Out of habit, we still split dinners out and we split grocery bills.

The necessity for separate accounts became very, very clear when Don got hit with a lawsuit. The suit covered everyone who had worked on a condo-apartment building project. He, the architect, was caught in a net with the contractor, the painters, the framers, the plumbers, etc. Everyone got sued. Eventually, as it should have been, he was not found at fault in anyway, but in the meantime, we had to hire a lawyer. The suit cost us about $50,000. At the center of this mess, I remember asking our attorney if demands could be placed on my business (since everyone else was getting sued!). He assured me it wouldn't happen. Thanks to the businesses clearly and visibly being separate, they couldn't go after Facèré (it is assumed if you have any kind of business with the word "jewelry" in it, that you have deep pockets, even when you're hustling to pay the next month's rent!).

Here's another important reason to keep your money separate: after you've covered the basic living costs together, you can spend your money any way you want! Don loves mechanical toys, I love collecting art. We can both splurge in our own way. My first marriage wasn't like that. In the first marriage, I took care of the money. It made me crazy when he'd buy a book for his book collection without checking to see if we'd paid the electricity bill! And now, if I want to buy clothes, it's my money, my choice. If he wants a new saw? I really don't care.

Employing Your Spouse

Don has become the website photographer for Facèrè Jewelry Art Gallery. He gets paid, just like any other employee, with a monthly paycheck, taxes all on the up and up. Tonight we need to repaint a couple of cases in the shop. Two hours of work on a dreadfully hot Sunday. I'll pay him and I'll take him to dinner.

Don used to pour champagne for each opening at Facèrè. At year twelve, he said, "enough!" Spouses need to be able to quit. Like any other employee.

More than Work

I try not to talk incessantly about work, or bring all my worries home. We counter the worries, concerns, successes about our businesses by attending Great Books, by going to the theatre, by attending openings and art auctions, by entertaining. I belong to a writing group which meets once a month. He built a boat, which took three years. In effect, we've created lives outside of our businesses.

If it should happen that...

Your spouse is your business partner, find at least three other couples who have shared a business partnership and ask for a couple hours of their time. Over lunch or dinner (that's three different occasions), come prepared to ask questions about how they have made it work (or haven't!).

Having a business partner has never appealed to me. I like being the boss. I like making decisions. I like shifting direction at any given moment. I like handling the consequences.

Should you need, for financial reasons, to have a partner or partners, with the help of your attorney, create a clear, written agreement that defines the duties and obligations of each partner. Anticipate the worst so you can create the best.

WORKBOOK CHAPTER SEVEN
DO MORE, DO IT BETTER

Touching Base

If you feel as if you are doing too much, find something more to do. I know that sounds mad, but somehow, for me, running a business has meant adding more. I don't get bored. And I don't have time to give up.

For instance, getting another degree. It was one of the best things I've ever done. It made me a more interesting person (at least I felt as if I had more to say, more to share). In retail, you meet a wide variety of people. If you understand "passion" (in this case painting), you can see what excites other people. You have a reference for understanding why someone collects toasters, or swizzle sticks, or colored diamonds. Or you have a reference for someone who loves jazz, or travels to Luca, or stands quietly in a stream fly-fishing. In the end, passion makes people connect and passion becomes the conversation.

I studied painting but I also salted my life with theatre, board work, poetry, music, art walks. It makes my life "more" and it allows for solid conversations with customers. Maybe not always. Maybe someone cuts me dead: "I'll let you know when I want assistance" said in the snippiest, nostril flared, you-are-just-a-clerk voice. Thank goodness, that is a rare moment. Most moments are friendly. Some moments involve a sale. Some don't. But the shared moments, when they happen, make for a better day. And once in awhile you *do* make a friend and, often enough, you make a sale.

Knowing When You Need Another Point of View

Thank goodness for small business consultants. Five times in the past forty years, I have hired Stephen Fletcher. Stephen consults with small businesses. I hired Stephen when I ran out of steam (when I had two locations).

A digression: have one location or seven locations, never have two locations. If you have two, plan immediately on the next five, otherwise stick with one. Two locations make for confusion and craziness.

Back to hiring a consultant. I needed Stephen particularly when retail disappeared during the dot.com bust, or at the beginning of the recession. But I also needed him when I made major moves:
- Renewed a lease
- Needed a larger line of credit
- Hired a new manager
- Opened a second location

There were always breaks between the times I hired

him. I highly recommend an outside point of view. The cost of the consultant always paid for itself.

Here are a few examples of ways in which the consultant worked with us:

Hiring

Stephen created a process for interviewing. From an ad in the newspaper, we interviewed six candidates. The first interview was very formal. We stood as the candidate entered the store. We shook hands with the candidate. We asked him or her to be seated. Stephen, Don, and I, sat across from the candidate in a row of chairs. We had a list of twenty questions, which we read to the candidate. We valued the answers numerically. The questions ranged from a general topic, such as, "Tell us about your education," to very specific topics, such as, "What is the last book you have read?"

The last question was always revealing: "What would you do if you received a call at work about an emergency at home?"

The range of questions allowed us to see how the person thought. With the last question we wanted to hear that whatever the answer, they would take care of both the gallery and the home emergency. We told each interviewee we would be in touch within two days.

And then there were three candidates.

In the second interview we set up a pretend selling situation with a piece of jewelry. The candidate had to sell the piece to Don. Stephen and I took notes. We watched to see how the candidate handled the jewelry. We watched to see how long it took the candidate to get the piece of jewelry in Don's hand. We watched for eye contact. We watched for the "ask" or the "close." Again we graded the candidate's responses.

We invited back two candidates.

We greeted each candidate warmly. We served coffee and cookies. We sat in a circle. The last interview was always the "telling" interview. The third interview clinched the choice. We asked casual questions, not reading them and not appearing to the candidate that we were taking score. We wanted the candidate to relax. We asked why they wanted the job. We asked what were his or her strongest skills and what skills would they be willing to expand. After we visited for awhile we asked, "Why should we hire you?"

In this last interview we listened for grammar, watched manners, concentrated on the ability of the person to be engaging.

Newsletter

The first newsletter was created by an advertising agency. Once again Stephen, Don, and I interviewed three agencies. In person. At their office. Choice was a combination of budget, product, and presentation. We wrote the newsletter and did the photographs, and then we gave it over to the agency.

Each newsletter cost one dollar. We mailed two hundred copies quarterly.

The end product was very finished: four-fold, historical research on antique jewelry, photos of customers at openings, and photos of new acquisitions.

Today, we create a two page newsletter in four colors and send it electronically.

To see past newsletters, visit the Facèré web site, click the ABOUT tab, and scroll down to Newsletters.

Board of Advisors

Why would anyone give up their precious time to advise a small business about what to do? Who would possibly be interested? The answers are in Chapter Seven: Thinking Big, Then Bigger.

I no longer have an advisory board, but the concept has not been lost. This last spring I invited a new neighbor who knows nothing about my business (but he does have a Doctorate from MIT, he's very young, and he has a wife who wears some jewelry). Because the economy has been very squirrelly, I offered to trade him whatever his hourly charge would be for two hours of analyzing my business. Rob was perfect! He spent way more than two hours and looked with great intent at our web site, at our store, how we worked with customers, and then met with the entire staff with two pages of notes. It was as if I had an advisory board of one. His recommendations were specific and useable. We are presently cleaning everything with great vigor. We've also adjusted our web site, to make tracking items easier. We've changed the introductory words in our literary magazine, *Signs of Life*. For all of his great work, I traded him two hours worth of merchandise. A great investment.

Pursuing the Big Guys

Going up-town in Seattle took months of persuasion. I "courted" the men at the Sheraton Hotel. The lesson for the reader: persistence, professionalism, and pleasantness. I never once lost the conviction that the hotel needed me. Stephen was by my side the entire time. Perhaps today it would not be quite so necessary, but having a business<u>man</u> in a business suit with great business sense, opened the way to the owners and manager of the Sheraton Hotel. I wore those men down. I also dropped $80,000 worth of improvements in their hotel. In the end, securing the hotel location paved the way for the City Centre space I now occupy. It was worth it.

WORKBOOK CHAPTER EIGHT
HAVING A GOOD TIME!

Giving a party

In 1984 I hired a publicity person and told him the advertising/promotion budget for the year was $30,000. He committed Facèré to $50,000. Yes, I wrote every check. My fault. But his ideas were so wonderful! So much fun! So extravagant!

Now I plan my own parties and knowing what I know, it is still difficult to stay on budget.

The perfect party is the one where you don't wonder if anyone is going to attend.
To assure attendance, the staff and I do the following:

Lectures

Before each opening we have a lecture. The lecture takes place in the boardroom on the fourth floor of our building. We invite three of the artists from the show to speak. They each have a twelve-to fifteen-minute presentation.

Why lectures? Lectures focus the attendees' attention on jewelry art. Lectures introduce artists to our customers and their images and words lead to an understanding of how and why they create jewelry art. When the lecture ends, forty-five to fifty people descend on the gallery and I don't have to worry if anyone is going to attend the party!

Champagne

What to serve is a budgetary decision. A person attending one of our earliest events had this to say: "You give such wonderful parties, and you serve such cheap champagne!" Well, when you're serving between forty-five and one-hundred pours in an evening, less expensive champagne is what is in the budget.

Most customers don't notice one way or another, but if one person did, then the rule of thumb is ten people did but didn't say anything but they also thought the champagne wasn't up to standards. We pay attention to customers' criticisms. Now I buy champagne that costs one dollar more than the cheap champagne, but it is a bottle with an unidentifiable label.

Taking the Party to the Streets

If you have a parade on city streets, you probably need a permit. But, if you are naïve and the parade happens to happen, and it's short, well then maybe you can get away with a New Orleans Brass Band and customers twirling colorful umbrellas walking a block and a half down the middle of town. We did. But I was asked after this particular party, by a city employee, "How did you do that?" We just did it. After which we served liquor.

Liquor

In Seattle, liquor laws are strict. We always pay for the city's banquet permit (which allows us to serve liquor). At every event I have a "greeter" who hands out two tickets to each attendee. "Hi! Welcome. Here are your drink tickets." That way we are in control of liquor consumption. And the reason we so carefully control consumption is due to the fact that one evening before we instigated the two-ticket rule, we had a woman drink too much. Not only had she had too much, she demanded a bottle of champagne to take home. She was on the edge of creating a scene, so we gave her a bottle. The experience was horrible. Enter the tickets. It's a way of saying "two drinks is the limit." For everyone.

We also instruct our "pourer" to pour light. Another way of controlling liquor.

Not to belabor the point, but in our state, and perhaps in yours, you are responsible for someone over-drinking and if he or she is in an accident, you, the host/hostess may be liable.

Give-aways

One of our most highly attended parties is our December Ornament Give-away. I invite all of my artists, around fifty, to create a single ornament for which I pay $40. The night of the party, which begins our holiday season, we give the ornaments away.

- Each ornament is displayed on a rack, with the name of the artist attached.
- To be in the drawing, participants must RSVP to the invitation sent two weeks before.
- The participant who wins must be present (not parking the car, not in the bathroom).
- Almost every ornament never sees a tree, but goes on the winner's body.
- As I present the ornament, I rave about the work and mention something distinctive and complimentary about the artist who made it.
- This is the evening when not much is sold, but choices are made and the following few days the phone rings with requests.

Pre-shopping

Pre-event. Before every show we tell as many people as possible to come in a day or two early to preview the show. Customers out of the area are encouraged to check the web site. Many pieces are sold prior to the opening night reception. Pre-selling is absolutely necessary to create an atmosphere of "must have!"

Picture Taking

Take pictures at every event. When the twenty-fifth anniversary comes around you can create a display showing all the people who've attended, all the artists you've featured. We also include these photos in our newsletters, between events.

Plan to spend more on the larger events. Budget well, but generously. Make what you do memorable. If the budget allows, have:

- Ice sculptures
- Live music
- A drawing for a major piece of jewelry
- Free parking (in our building that is a memorable gift!)
- Name tags
- Special treats (It is not unusual for one of my wonderful staff to make treats that represents something in the show, e.g. once Susan made brownies with the image of Charles Lewton-Brain on each piece. Charles was one of the artists in the show and his image adorned one of his pieces of jewelry.)
- Book signings

Etc., etc., etc: take chances…you want people talking the next day and you want the evening to be festive. But don't forget your budget.

What NOT to do

- Don't have a Men's Only evening on the night of a football game.

- Create a game (see right), that is so difficult it frustrates your customers.

Building A Business, Building A life

THE FACÈRÈ ♥ALENTINE

A Celebration To Sweethearts! You Are Invited To This Sale, Competition, Game and Party.

THE FACÈRÈ HEART GAME

The clues which are on the left are names, songs, movies, etc. Write your answer in the correct space on the right.

Please bring this invitation and heart game when you attend the Valentine Party, February 6, 6:00 p.m. at Facèrè Jewelry Art.

1. ♥ T ♥ (EXAMPLE) — Heart to Heart
2. M♥ - M, M♥ - M — Mary Hartman, Mary Hartman
3. S, ♥OTIE — Spokane, Heart OF the Inland Empire
4. M♥BTD — My Heart Belongs to Daddy
5. 2♥BAO — 2 Hearts Beat As One
6. WASIM♥ — With A Song In My Heart
7. ♥zMBS — Hartz Mt. Bird Seed
8. ML♥s — Miss Lonely hearts
9. J♥ — Jawilk Heart
10. POM♥ — Peg o' My Heart
11. RA♥ — Rogers And Hart
12. COT♥ — Crimes of the Heart
13. ♥LAW — Heart Like A Wheel
14. B♥d (or) B♥d — Broken hearted or Big Hearted
15. ♥OMS — Heart ON My Sleeve
16. K♥AC — Kind Hearts And Coronets
17. YDSOM♥ASTSF — ✱
18. ♥SAM — Hart Schaffner And Marx
19. ILM♥ISF — I Left My Heart iN S.F.
20. 2♥sI¾T — 2 Hearts iN 3/4 Time

Each day, beginning January 29, we will give out a new answer, but not by telephone! Come see us, we'll present our new designers, the Valentine Show of Northwest Artists and provide all you need to give a wonderful, lasting gift for Valentine's Day (...and of course, the answer).

✱ You Done Stomped ON My Heart And Squashed That Sucker Flat!

FEB 1987

Building A Business, Building A life

- Inside every invitation to the grand opening at the Sheraton Hotel, we included a ruby. Two hundred rubies were synthetic. Five rubies were real. Everyone was to come into the gallery to have their stone checked to see if they had received one of the real rubies.

Guess what? Twenty people came in. Not real. They left disappointed. Not one person brought in the $200 rubies. I guess they got thrown out with the garbage! That was one of my really bad ideas.

- There are probably many more Not to Do's that I've suppressed. Too painful to remember.

One last thought about parties: Remember to have a good time. Your most important job at special events is to schmooze with as many people as possible. You're the host/hostess. Your guests are in your "living room." What you're selling at a party is a good time.

WORKBOOK CHAPTER NINE
FALLING IN LOVE WITH A SPACE

I fell in love with every space I've ever occupied. Some of those spaces didn't return my investment (of love and money!).

I wish someone had given me the following list and had I had such a list I would have paid attention to the answers. You'll need to add your own particular questions. But before you hone in on any particular spaces for consideration, do this: go to three of your favorite retail locations. List everything you like. Note what isn't working (from your point of view).

Checklist for a retail location

1. Size

_____ Square footage: how much do you envision you will need?
_____ Floor plan: what will make the customer walk by every case, every display?
_____ Wall space: how much do you need and how will you use it?
_____ Given the size you are considering, how many people will you need to service the customers and deter shoplifting?

_____ Consider your merchandise: how much small space do you need? How much large space do you need? How many different artists, different kinds of merchandise, do you need to attract customers to your space?

2. Signage/Visibility

_____ How far a distance will your signs be visible (outside signs and inside signs)?
_____ Will your building require you to pay extra for signage?
_____ Will your signage need landlord approval?
_____ What two to three words (under the name of your business) explain what you are selling?
_____ If someone drives by, will your location be identifiable?
_____ If your location is not on the street, is there signage outside that will direct customers inside?
_____ When you are closed, what kind of window displays will you have for after-hour perusing?
_____ What kind of signage fits your space and fits your image: Neon? Painted? Three-dimensional? Back-lit? And, if your signage requires electricity, is wiring available?

3. Street traffic/Foot traffic/Parking

_____ What is the noise level of street traffic?
_____ What is the distance to parking? What is the cost

Building A Business, Building A life

of parking? Will you have any free parking?

_____ Set aside an hour in the morning and an hour in the afternoon to do a count of foot traffic. As you do your foot traffic count, indicate the age of the people walking by. Are they your customers?

_____ How visible is the location? Corner location? Mid-block? Will your retail neighbors compliment your business?

_____ Is your space wheelchair accessible?

_____ Will you be able to leave your front door open?

_____ Is there a bus stop in front of your location (a difficult barrier)?

List all of the retail shops in a three-block radius. Visit each. What do you estimate the average sale might be?

_____ Are the other retail shops competitors?

_____ If the other retailers are competitors, how will you be different?

_____ Do the other retail shops compliment your business?

_____ Any hotels? Restaurants? Businesses that bring repeat customers?

4. Security

_____ Will you need to have a safe? How big? What degree of fireproof will your safe require? If you require a safe for your business, you will need to know your insurance company's requirements for the size of safe, the hours it is fire proof, the extensiveness of an alarm system, and the possibility of a panic button for immediate access to the police department.

_____ If someone were to rob your store, are there natural barriers between your most valuable merchandise and an exit?

_____ For safety, do you have room for at least two sales persons at all times?

_____ What kind of guards or watchmen might you require? Does your landlord supply such services? And if so, what is the additional cost to your lease?

5. Entrance

_____ Double door? Single door?
_____ Well lit?
_____ Welcoming?
_____ Do window displays at your entrance lead the customer into the shop?

6. Amenities

_____ How close is the nearest drinking fountain or coffee shop?
_____ How close is the nearest bank?
_____ Is there an ATM close by for your customers?
_____ Where is the closest public restroom?
_____ If there are steps, is there also a ramp?
_____ If you need it, are there additional storage facilities to rent for your supplies?
_____ Is there a space for you to conduct lectures?

Have staff meetings?
_____ Is there an area for parties and openings?

7. Landlord/Space

_____ Who owns your retail space? Is there any chance you could own it some day? Might it be for sale right now? Will owners allow you to sublet your space?

_____ What retail experience do the owners of your space have?

_____ On the owner's staff, who will be your contact person?

_____ How long a lease do you want or do they require? Will the lease be renewable? What are the conditions of either extending or ending a lease agreement?

_____ Who builds-out the tenant improvements? At what cost? Who will design the space? Will the designer and contractor work with you directly?

You will be adding your own questions to this list. This is a work-sheet to get you started in the difficult and challenging process of choosing a location. Happy hunting!

WORKBOOK CHAPTER TEN
CROOKS, THIEVES, SCAMMERS AND THINGS THAT GO BUMP IN THE NIGHT

A Knight in Shining Armor

When I opened my business, it never crossed my mind that someone, someday, would have to save my business. It never crossed my mind that there were predators, crooks, scammers, slight-of-hand thieves, felons, bad-check writers, and every kind of malfeasant-type in between. It never crossed my mind that "evil" could be so immediate and so devastating. It wasn't that I didn't know about crooks, thieves, scammers, and things that go bump in the night. Anybody who reads the morning paper knows life has its big depressions. I just never thought anyone would want to take away my business.

And accomplices...

Besides the incident where I was rescued, I am sorry to say all of the following have happened in my business:

- Bad-check writers set us up with two small purchases on two different days. The third shopping trip they bought two rings and wrote a check for seven hundred dollars. It took ten days before the bank returned the check with "Closed Account" stamped across its face.

We had an address. We had a phone number. We never found them, even though we went to the skid road apartment address where they had once resided. We called the bank where they worked. The bank told us all of the employee information was confidential.

"Even when your employees are crooks?"
"Yes." Conversation over.

We made a police report (always make a police report if for no other reason it will make you feel less a victim).

And the outcome? They completely got away.

- The slight-of-hand artist entered with his girl friend. She was chatty and delightful while he slipped a wire from inside his sleeve into a case with the teeniest crack. I looked over just in time to see a diamond bracelet suspended in mid-air. I screamed at him and the two of them fled. This happened early on in my career, before I knew to call 911. Today? I call at the slightest provocation.

- A traveling salesman sold me a pair of earrings with an "appraisal." Nothing about what was written was true, except that they were earrings. That was the very last time I trusted an appraisal done by any other than the gemologists we work with. The scammer? Never saw him again.

- We are "cased" regularly. Usually young. Usually dopey. Easy to recognize after all these years. The last idiot came into the gallery just a few days ago. He was so young and so dopey, that when he said, "This was my grandmother's," I sternly "advised" him to get a different opening line because every dumb kid with a piece of stolen merchandise starts with that line! "It was my grandmother's" is code for "I've got a deal for you!" I was still lecturing him as he walked out the door.

- Over the years, credit card theft has become the easy theft. No matter how careful we might be, there is that one person who chitter-chats all through the sale, flashes an ID, gains your confidence, and you forget to be skeptical, or you forget to match signatures closely, or you think, well, that photo ID isn't quite right, but this person is smiling! Those mistakes? You pay for them.

- And all of those items that just disappear:
  An $8000 gold and ruby necklace
  An antique gold ball locket with seven compartments
  An 18k solid gold chain worth $2000

You're in retail? Thefts are referred to as "shrinkage." Items shrink to itsy-bitsy nothingness and over the years I continue to hunt for those missing pieces. Did we check every single box in the workroom? Did we look on every single shelf? Maybe, somehow, mysteriously, is it inside a book? Caught inside an umbrella? Our search becomes more imaginative and more futile.

The search never ends.

After forty years I still can't believe someone would steal from us.

So, beware. If you are in business, the crooks of the world will find you. When the big one comes along, maybe a Knight in Shining Armor will be there to help save you.

What to do about rounding up Knights in Shining Armor?

Define your Knight

- Established
- Visible
- Known for "giving back to the community"
- Accessible: what is the possibility if you were to call and ask him/her to go to coffee, he/she would say yes? If there is a 50% chance the answer would be yes, put that person on your list.
- Powerful: is your knight that person? Or does he or she know the person you need to know?

Where you might find Knights

- Chamber of Commerce
- Better Business Bureau
- Rotary
- International Society of Appraisers, local chapter
- National Jewelry Appraisers, local chapter
- GIA and local chapter of GIA
- Metals Guild, national and local
- Business Owners Association
- Downtown Association
- Kiwanis

- Jewelry Historians
- Women Business Owners
- Leadership Tomorrow

Determine which organizations you will join

- Who is on the board of directors?
- How much attention does the group pay to small business?
- What kinds of activities do they sponsor?
- If you join, will you have at least one activity a month to attend?
- Can you afford the dues?
- Will you be expected to give financially above and beyond the dues?
- How much time and energy do you have to give?

Attend an event as a prospective member

- Were you able to meet at least five other business owners?
- Did you find out how to access a committee?
- Would they want you on a committee?
- Whatever this group stands for, can you support it?
- Were their businesses similar in size and spirit to yours?
- Did you introduce yourself to the chairperson? The organizer? The speaker?
- Did you exchange cards with other attendees? Twenty cards given and received?

Join

I chose The Chamber of Commerce. I also joined The International Society of Appraisers, The National Association of Jewelry Appraisers, Jewelry Historians, Women Business Owners, and was accepted in to Leadership Tomorrow. I did not think, "I'll join the Chamber because the most powerful people in the city belong." I was too naïve to have such a thought. But when I joined the Chamber of Commerce, it was immediately apparent that this was one of those organizations in Seattle where the powerful men and women congregated.

As a new member of the Chamber, I attended meetings and lectures that were relevant to my business in size, employees, goals. Shortly thereafter, I joined the Small Business Committee. We planned programs and invited speakers to inspire and inform us. Not that much later I was the chair of the committee. Being the chair expanded my contacts. Once a month all of the committee chairs met to report on their activities. I went prepared and dressed for the occasion (this was the time when *Dress for Success* was the bible to which one subscribed. I had a closet full of suits).

After being the chair for two years, an invitation came my way. A very important invitation. The invitation was to join "The President's Club." This was an organization that supported the President of the Chamber of Commerce and was responsible for bringing corporate members into the chamber. As I recall, at that time only two women had ever, in the history of the club, been invited to join. I jumped at the chance.

I worked hard and when Herb Bridge became President of the Chamber, he was a person I could call for coffee. When the day came that I truly needed him, I called. He came to the rescue.

In Conclusion

So ends or begins the story of how to secure the friendships that you might someday need to save your business. In the process, you will have become acquainted with how businesses of all sizes survive and you, perhaps, will be in a position to be that Knight in Shining Armor for someone else.

And the Beat Goes On

Herb's business, Ben Bridge Jewelers, a chain of over twenty-eight stores, was purchased by Warren Buffet. Shortly after, I called Herb for coffee. I proposed to him that Mr. Buffet might want to buy Facèré and create a chain of small jewelry art galleries to serve as the "cutting edge" for their more traditional chain. I suggested that they might hire me for such an expansion.

Herb thought the idea had merit and ran it by Buffet.

He reported back to me that Buffet didn't think the

idea had that much merit. Why? It wouldn't be profitable for a long, long, long time.

Given how much Warren Buffet knows about investing, he was probably right. But I think he missed a great opportunity to have a lot of fun!

And…

The visibility of the business owner is as important as the visibility of the business. In the case of most small businesses, the business is the owner, the owner the business. Being active in the group or groups you decide to join is absolutely essential. Join a committee. Attend events. Have your business card ready. The key word is "active."

WORKBOOK CHAPTER ELEVEN
LETTERS AND LESSONS

I was pleased and rather surprised when, while sorting through piles of drafts of my short stories, essays, and novels, I stumbled upon the correspondence with Gary Carpenter and Dick Clotfelter, reprinted in Chapter 11, "I Think I'm Going to Slit My Wrists." I don't recall thinking it would be wise or useful or in any way important to keep these letters. It wasn't as if they were saved, it was more that they weren't thrown away. Those letters and the negotiations they referred to as I worked to obtain the treasured kiosk at Century Square, led to the following lessons:

Keeping records

- Keep all correspondence.
- Keep daily phone logs, with dates and synopsis of conversations.
- Keep a copy of your lease.
- Keep a photo record of construction, empty and occupied spaces, parties, important customers. (Had I been very smart, these pages would now be spiced with photographs of Meg Ryan, Dennis Hopper, the Smothers Brothers, Curt Cobain and Courtney Love. And only because a friend was handy, did I get a picture of Prince Andrew!)

Building A Business, Building A life

And why should you keep this full, fat paper trail? Because some day you just might want to write the history of your business. I never thought I would ever attempt to reconstruct the past forty years of retail. Had I kept more of everything, this assignment would have been much easier.

You think you'll remember? Believe me, no matter how many blueberries you eat, your memory will grow dim and you will want all of the reminders you can possibly store.

Mind Your Manners

More than likely, over time you will negotiate with a number of landlords. As a business person, even if you only negotiate a lease every five years, it is important to remain cordial, business-like, clear, precise, humble, and sweetly demanding. Which is also a reason to take your lawyer or your business advisor or your accountant with you, someone who will be the calming element, in case you lose it.

I lost it once. Horribly. I was not cordial or business-like, and I was very demanding. I regret it to this day (ten years later). I can't even remember what brought about the anger. I do, however, remember where it happened and with whom. I'll skip those two details, as our relationship has since been restored. Here's a snapshot of what happened:

    I stormed into my landlord's office with no semblance of containment or rationality.

I remember the receptionist cringing when I demanded to see someone. Anyone! I demanded someone appear from the back office. Right now!

When the person in charge appeared, I went so far as to demand, "What in the F___ is going on!" Indeed. I used the F word.

I got immediate attention. The person I demanded to see stood astounded and then that person's boss appeared and the two of them ushered me into a conference room and they closed the door.

They listened to my rant.

Very calmly the building manager asked what I wanted to have happen (this is a brilliant strategy if ever you are on the other side of such a stupid confrontation).

I told them that I thought a little more communication between us would certainly help matters—perhaps something so obvious and simple (I was still ranting) as quarterly meetings with the business owners in the building.

They agreed that that was not an unreasonable request.

We shook hands all around.

I left.

Anger dissipated.

Nothing much ever came of the idea of having quarterly meetings with the retail tenants.

Here's what did happen: ever since, when we meet, there is an edge of groveling on my part. I have been making up for my unmannerly outburst ever since. Believe me, losing it does not put you in a power position. So, don't do what I did, unless you are ready

Building A Business, Building A life

to pack it in, break your lease, and have their lawyers demanding rent for how ever long your broken lease states.

So, to summarize: don't lose your cool; don't yell; don't use the F word or any other permutation of disrespect.

You want something to happen?
- Put it in writing.
- Put the written request in a drawer.
- In a day or two, take out that draft and rewrite it.
- Be specific and clear about your requests.
- Save the correspondence, your requests, and their answers.
- Call ahead for an appointment.
- Call another professional, e.g., the lawyer, business advisor, or accountant to join you.
- Present your request precisely and simply.
- Back at your business, send a memo recapping the salient points of your meeting (ending with a thank-you is a wise strategy).
- One month later, revisit the correspondence file and see if any of your requests were met.
- If <u>anything</u> has been accomplished, send another memo acknowledging the progress and sign-off with another thank-you.
- Continue this strategy until your requests have been met.
- Your success rate will give you a clue about what you might expect in the lease negotiations.

Now let's talk about negotiating a lease.

Lease negotiations are rare. In thirty-eight years I have negotiated a new lease three times and renegotiated my current lease twice. You'll need the help of your attorney and if he is not available to accompany you to the negotiations (or you can't afford to have him accompany you), take your business consultant (generally less costly than the attorney) and if you don't have either at the time you are negotiating, take your accountant. Take someone! You need an extra pair of ears and you need to look as if you have "your people" on board. There is power in numbers even if it is two.

Begin negotiating no less than six months before you occupy a space or the present lease expires. If you are renegotiating because of some kind of emergency (such as a major recession!), less time might work and might be necessary. Which ever, you need time to digest the lease and your attorney needs time to approve.

Once, when cash flow was the problem, I made an exception. I went to the landlord's office alone. I needed to look needy (it wasn't difficult to do). I took bookwork showing the drop in sales. The landlord was not unaware, as I report sales every month. But, here's the interesting part. I got what I wanted. A major reduction in rent. They got what they wanted. A lease extension. And they increased the percentage of sales I would owe on the last five years of the extension. They don't call them LAND LORDS for nothing! They didn't lose. I got some breathing space. I'm now facing a percentage increase that will strain cash flow once again. Next time, I'll take my business consultant or I'll take all the paperwork to the attorney before I sign. Because this session was more casual, I treated it more casually. In the end I didn't calculate how much the increase in rent would be once the crisis passed. I don't resent the landlord's negotiations, but I think I could have negotiated smarter terms if I'd had professional help.

Professional Help

Learn to recognize when you need professional help.

Here's when:
- You negotiate or renegotiate a lease (your lawyer).
- Sales have dropped precipitously and you are on the edge of panic (your business advisor).
- You have someone threatening you such as the blustery customer who says, "I'm going to have my husband contact you! HE is an ATTORNEY!" You need to have someone tell you to relax. Once, and only once, to an angry, abusive customer, my attorney wrote a letter stating the person would be trespassing should they ever enter my establishment again. She didn't.
- If you are a corporation, by law, at least in Washington State, you have to meet at least once a year with your board and your attorney (and your attorney can be on your board).
- Quarterly taxes, corporate taxes, any taxes (your accountant and your bookkeeper).
- When you've have a great success (newspaper coverage, perhaps), be sure all the professional people you work with receive a copy.

WORKBOOK CHAPTER TWELVE
ANSWERING/AVOIDING THE CUSTOMER'S UNANSWERABLE QUESTIONS

1. Take the initiative. Speak first!

After greeting the customer (make eye contact!), say something as simple as:
- "How's it going?"
- "How have you been?" (To a returning customer)
- "Don't forget there are more pieces in the drawers."
- "Ask if you have any questions!"
- "It must be raining again!" (If they are brushing off raindrops.)

These greetings help you determine just how much the customer needs your attention, at that moment, later, or not at all.

2. And the next bit of information

You will want to help the customer focus (we have many items in a small space, and helping the customer focus helps, perhaps, to make a sale).

We explain to the customer:

- Who we sell: "We represent over fifty jewelry artists from around the world."

- What we sell: "Almost all the pieces are one of a kind or limited edition."
- What more to learn: "The cards will tell you who the artist is, where they're from, and states the price range."
- How to view the jewelry art: "Each artist has a different style, different materials, a different message. Make yourself at home (at this point we open a drawer to show the customer that there is more to be viewed). And please ask if you have any questions."

3. Watch body language

At a certain point, it is important to address the customer. Usually that moment is indicated by body language. Watch to see when a customer leans into the case, twists his or her head to see a price, or looks directly at you to see if you are paying attention. Here are some greetings that let your customer know you are there when needed:

- "Ask if you wish to touch."
- "If you'd like to see how something is made, I'd be glad to show you."
- "I know you've purchased gifts before (when you are on firm ground with a past customer). I'll gladly check the computer to see what was successful."

4. No sale today?

If you begin to understand a person has shown interest, but there will be no sale, be sure to say something as he or she leaves, such as:

- "Check our web site. Here's our card."
- "This is an invitation to our next show."
- "Have a great day!"

5. Special shows

Many, many people who enter the gallery have never seen a piece of jewelry art in their lives. Explaining who and what we are is a challenge, but it is even more difficult when we have a show. Our greeting changes and as the customer is walked a few steps between cases, here are suggestions garnered from what we've said in the past:

- "You've come at a great time! This is a special show that opened last Wednesday. Nine different artists, around the theme of _____ (whatever the theme is), are here for just a few days (you are telling the customer this is a very special opportunity that won't be here for long)."

- And then we step back from the customer and add, "Don't forget the drawers; we have over fifty artists in addition to the show."

After the customer has a little time and space to look, engage them again:

- "Be sure to ask if you have any questions!" (To which the answer is almost always "Thank-you," and rarely, rarely "I'm just looking" which is a way of putting you in your place, you clerk you!)

Building A Business, Building A life

I must admit that if someone DEMANDS to be left alone (by a look, by a cold shoulder, by totally ignoring a greeting), they should be left alone. There are people who let you know with no doubt that they want you to exit! If that is the case, let them be! I've a jillion things to do and I go do them. But, from behind the counter I watch the customer's body language, because sometimes that grouchy customer leans over a case, tilts their head at an angle that could possibly cause muscle spasms, and I'm right there ready to say:

- "Let me open that case so you can see better!" With a smile, and with the key out, and undeterred, I open the case. I pick up the piece they have been straining to see and offer it to them.

Sometimes, their response is, "No, no, no, I'm *really* just looking," and I've been known to say, "It's okay! It's my job!!" There isn't much "no" left in the recalcitrant customer after that.

Then there is the wrong customer in the wrong shop at the wrong time and if they freeze me out, and I haven't energy or attitude, I say, "Sure nuf!" and go back to writing letters and making phone calls and answering emails to real customers who love Facèrè and love jewelry art.

Fair warning. There have been "wrong" customers in the "wrong" shop and I compliment their jewelry (which is only done if it deserves complimenting), or I read their name tag and see they are from Chicago (where I once lived), or they are wet with rain, and I make the appropriate comment, and a half-hour later they leave chatty and smiling and it has been a lovely interchange and maybe they'll come back, or maybe they won't, but I've turned a sour moment sweet.

Don't give up! Most people are wonderful and worth the time you give them (and they give you!). Always remember, your shop is your at-work living room and they are your guests!

And for the inappropriate questions as described in Chapter Twelve, remember, you don't have to answer them.

6. Educating the customer

- Identification cards with each artist's work with name, degrees, short description and price range.
- In our monthly newsletter we feature our artist's accomplishments (go to the web site, hit ABOUT, and check out past newsletters).
- With every purchase of jewelry, no matter how inconsequential, we give the buyer a "portfolio" about the artist whose work they have purchased. With the portfolio is a letter explaining why they have received the information (they have joined the world of jewelry art collecting). In addition, we include an article about the gallery, the resumé of the artist, an artist's statement, and if available, an article from an art publication about the artist.

Over the years we have given away hundreds of these portfolios. The additional information enhances the buyer's collection. The additional information increases the perceived value of the purchase.

We at Facèré believe it is our obligation to grow the field of jewelry art and to enhance the careers of our artists. The cards, the newsletter, and the portfolio are ways of accomplishing our goal.

7. The positive attitude of selling

- Remember to smile.
- Find the compliment…and make it!
- Remember your gallery is like your home. Be courteous even if it is someone asking directions to the bathroom.
- Have fun.

WORKBOOK CHAPTER THIRTEEN
TAKING ADVANTAGE OF OPPORTUNITIES

Growing opportunities

Opportunities happen, and if you are quick to grab them, doors open.
- Learn to say yes more often than you say no
- Take chances
- Prepare

1. I turned down an opportunity that only came once. I was offered two weeks study at Centrum in Port Townsend, Washington, with Cy Twonbly, a noted painter. Somehow I didn't think I had time or money. In truth, I had both, but I didn't make it happen. I could have borrowed the money. I could have found a house sitter for my dogs. I could have taken a much needed vacation from my business. Years later I visited the Twombly Museum in Houston, and realized how beautiful and profound his work is, and it hit me how much I had missed by saying "no" when I should have said "yes."

2. If you think you would rather die than say yes to a public speaking engagement, change your mind. You won't die. You'll be nervous. You might forget a few words or say too many "ummms." Take the

nervousness and turn it into the energy it is. Accept every speaking opportunity offered, even if it is as simple as toasting Uncle Jack at a family dinner or as challenging as a television audience of thousands. You'll learn to love that nervous energy and speaking engagements help grow your business.

3. Preparation comes in many forms:

- Toastmasters groups abound. Check in your area for a group, and join. Toastmasters is inexpensive and meets regularly. With a small supportive and gently critical group you will get a variety of speaking experiences and you will become the speaker you always wished to be.

- Take classes in public speaking at your local community college or university extension program. An academic class will probably be more rigorous and more challenging. If nothing else it will be different and you will have invested more money, and one would assume, more energy.

4. Appraising is a job all of its own. There are national organizations who offer programs and certification. Check The International Society of Appraisers (ISA); or The National Association of Jewelry Appraisers (NAJA); or The American Association of Appraisers (AAA). These programs cost time and money, but if you wish to appraise, you need the credentials.

Often such organizations have local chapters. Joining and participating will give you other speaking opportunities and will keep you up-to-date on appraising, especially necessary for federal tax donation appraisals.

5. Local television, radio, and newspapers need to be courted. Regularly send news releases. Regularly recommend story ideas to the media. Regularly recommend stories about your colleagues, your associates, and your business neighbors. This is especially true once you have been interviewed. Keep in touch with that writer/reporter with ideas other than ideas about your business. Send a simple hand-written note. Or send an e-mail. Continue to let the media know you are thinking of them.

6. Getting national coverage is more difficult, but not impossible. Work the field like you would your local media. Every year I send Scott Simon, host of *Weekend Edition* on National Public Radio, a copy of the literary magazine we publish, *Signs of Life*. He hasn't acknowledged its existence yet, but there's no reason not to continue trying.

7. I didn't turn down an unusual opportunity to serve on a national board (The Society of North American Goldsmiths). When I was asked to run for the board, I hesitated and then instead of saying "No" as a number of friends and a husband had suggested might be the right answer, I decided to say yes. For the next three years I believe I will learn more about my field than just about any other thing I could have chosen to say yes to.

8. One of the most rewarding bits recently happened when we gave away a copy of *ABeCeDarian* (2011). I delivered a copy of our book to the Montessori School in our building. With it was a note to say, "I thought your children might enjoy this book."

The next day, two five-year olds, accompanied by their teacher, arrived at our shop with a very large thank-you card, signed by all the children.

I have no idea where or if this connection will result in anything more than their cheerful voices calling, "Thank you! Thank you!" as they left.

The happiness (and near tears) it brought me was more than worth the gift.

WORKBOOK CHAPTER FOURTEEN
PUTTING IT IN WRITING

Writing and speaking

Two activities connected to business which cannot be avoided are writing and speaking.

- Write a business plan—you are going to have to show the plan to your banker, your business consultant, your possible partner. To begin, copy a good business plan that someone else has written (on line or at your local book store; a dozen books are available with business plans).

- Immediately begin adapting the plan to the ideas that make you stay awake at night—the good, positive ideas: what you will sell, where you'll be located, what it will cost. (Oops, that last idea is not for the middle of the night. Leave money planning for bright, sunny days, when anything is possible.)

- Start your own business history. Even if you don't want to publish a book, your kids, your great aunt, your parents will love to read your memories. Building a business is a great story!

Learning how to write

1. Don't believe because you can read, or love to read, that you can write. Writing is a craft to be learned. Learning to write well takes time and energy. And with time and energy, you'll learn to love rewriting. Find a place to learn.

2. Writing classes abound. If you think you aren't good at writing, you can become good. Check your local community college writing programs or, if one is nearby, consider a university's extension program. My experience with these kinds of classes has been very positive.

3. Colleges and universities tend to attract serious, often more mature writers. The classes I attended were filled with doctors, engineers, architects, salespersons, who had daytime jobs, who couldn't return to school fulltime, and who had a passion for writing.

4. Join a writing group. The writing group I attend has been in existence for sixteen years. I depend on this close group of writers for encouragement and writing practice (see Natalie Goldberg's, *Writing Down the Bones*, for suggestions on writing practice).

5. Getting someone to publish your writing is as difficult as the writing itself. You might want to start with pursuing business magazines. You'll learn all about rejections. However, not to worry if your initial attempts are rejected. Write about your business

experiences in a crisp, focused approach. Even if your attempts are rejected, you might stir interest in what you are doing, and a publication might send a reporter your way. My first national coverage in *Working Woman* (1983) happened because a daughter of an East Coast writer was seated in her sociology class next to a daughter of a customer. She was asked, "Do you know a woman business owner in Seattle?" She answered that she didn't, but that her mother did. Two days later I received a phone call from New York and two months later I was featured in the magazine. Serendipity. That's how articles often happen.

6. We have chosen at Facèré to publish-on-demand. I've had an agent. I've had limited success in literary magazines. What is sure-fire, is that when I self-publish, I have the book or magazine in my hand. Selling? Selling is a topic and a challenge all of its own.

7. Merchandising your writing:

- Begin with sending your writing to literary magazines. Check the internet. You will find a multitude of literary magazines to which you can submit. Check submission guidelines and follow them explicitly.
- If you self-publish, send ten to twenty free copies to the media. Send half to local media. Send half to national media.
- We publish books and our magazine in conjunction with a jewelry art show. When we can afford to do so, we give free copies to the artists involved. We give a free copy to those who purchase work from the show,

and we attempt to sell the rest. In the gallery there is a wall for publications. Not always, but once in awhile, the cost of the printing is covered by sales. However, the publicity the publications garner is worth the cost of publishing.

8. Writing and publishing are good for business. The sense of accomplishment is palpable. The books are a record of good times and good shows.

WORKBOOK CHAPTER FIFTEEN
FILLING THE TANK

Expanding Busy

Having a life separate from your business is essential to a healthy frame of mind, and strangely enough, it is good for business. This separate side is essential. Sometimes these activities are as consuming and demanding as the business. The activities that have sustained me include:
- Obtaining a second degree in painting
- Taking writing classes
- Getting qualified to appraise jewelry
- Traveling to Italy, Spain, Germany, Portugal, Mexico, and England
- Working on arts boards, both local and national
- Becoming a competent skier
- Playing baseball with the Serbo-Croatian University of Washington intramural baseball team
- Learning Greek dancing
- Trying to learn Italian and failing miserably

These activities have given me ideas, energy, and direction that stoke the fires and fill the tank.

One hundred things I want to do before I die

    Make a list.

Building A Business, Building A life

I started to make a list of things I wanted to do, and I had to stop because the exercise was making mystomach hurt. This is the same feeling I get when Suzie Orman says to honor your money by not leaving it in the pockets of your coats. I tried doing that. I hated it. I love finding money in my pockets.

You need to follow the words of the guru who make sense to you.

Better to make up your own goals. Maybe you want to only have five items on your list. But say "yes" to something! And remember to say "yes" to opportunities more often than you say "no."

And read….read widely and often. Recently we returned from our yearly Great Books weekend. We read four books I might never have picked up, including: *The Dead* by Joyce and *The Things They Carried* by Tim O'Brien. All four books were challenging. All the discussions were stimulating.

As you make your list, you'll be surprised at how busy life can be. Other activities to consider:

- Leadership Tomorrow (most cities have this program through their Chamber of Commerce)
- Get a dog—Sam our wonderful rescue dog introduces us to the neighborhood
- Water aerobics, bicycling, lifting weights, etc.
- Attending local festivals (in Seattle there is Bumbershoot and the Folklife Festival)

And why?

A variety of activities are important to running a business because:

- You have something to talk about with your customers.
- You have something to think about besides the hard stuff—like bills, the recession, the disappeared piece of jewelry, etc., etc.
- You build your body so that you can stand six hours a day.
- You are doing something besides working.

I love work. I love the gallery. I would love it only half as much if it were the only thing that filled my life.

Stumbling into opportunities

- Be alert to the unexpected. Follow your bliss. You've heard that expression a dozen times. It is one of those clichés that just happens to be bedded in truth. However, it might take half a lifetime to determine what's "bliss."

- Many collectors have opened galleries. Many artists have done the same. Many a jeweler tired of craft shows and street fairs, but still loved creating what they were creating, decided on bricks and mortar. If you are one of those, if you are exhausted and tired of being in the corporate world where you don't control your destiny or have done street fairs for long enough, look at the possibility of opening your own gallery.

And if you do....

- Determine how you are unique and translate that into how the gallery you create is unique.
- Niche is everything—what you do and how you present it and eventually, how you sell it, will define your uniqueness.
- If you create a space and fill it with merchandise that reflects your choices, your "eye," you will create your own niche.
- Sell yourself. Your ads, your space, and even your personal attire will speak to your identity.

Recently I attended a homeowner's event. I wore the simplest of necklaces: bright colored discs made from food container tops from a jewelry artist in Amsterdam. At least ten people noticed it. They spoke to me about it. It's my necklace. It is not for sale. But the idea of jewelry art as a saleable item was inherent in my very presence. The necklace? $83. The advertising by wearing it? Priceless.

WORKBOOK CHAPTER SIXTEEN
FINDING AND NURTURING ARTISTS OR
BEING FOUND AND BEING NURTURED

Finding/Being Found

There was a time when twenty-four artists in the gallery seemed the capacity for Facèré. Today we represent fifty artists and we have five shows a year where we invite outside artists. Special show invitations usually have a theme and last two to three weeks. We also show one or two student artists each summer.

How do we choose our artists? How might you be chosen?

- Artists often call for an appointment. An artist is coming to Seattle, has studied the web site, has a body of work to show, and needs representation on the West Coast. Chances are slim of being given a contract, but we never turn down the opportunity to look at new work. If coincidently the work is fresh, beautifully crafted, something like nothing else in the gallery, *and* at the moment we see it we have lost one of our artists for the usual reasons (change of career, pregnancy, exhaustion, whatever), we have on occasion immediately asked an artist to join us.

- The majority of artists contact us through the internet.

Again, the artists have studied the web site and he or she asks to be considered. We study the artist's website (it is rare an artist does not have a website), and perhaps ten or fifteen times a month we send a "No thank-you" response. Once in a great while we ask artists to send a small sampling of their work so that we can see the craftsmanship. Not to be discouraging, but the internet is the least affective way to approach the gallery.

- Occasionally artists featured in books or magazines draw our attention. Because of these articles and photos, we have solicited artists for special shows. This is a reason for all artists to enter competitions or to respond to calls to submit. Especially useful for Facèré has been the *Lark* books, *Ornament, Metalsmith,* and *American Craft* magazines.

- Shows of jewelry art at the Society of North American Goldsmith's (SNAG) Conference are another way for artists to get exposure.

- The Portfolio Review at the SNAG Conference has brought us student work for a summer contract. Again, this was serendipity. Students sign up for the Portfolio Review to have the opportunity to talk to a professional about the presentation of their artist statement, their resumé, and images of their work. Occasionally students bring a sampling of their work (five to ten pieces) to the review. Twice I invited two different students to be in touch after the conference. They received a summer contract. Showing with Facèré from June to September gives students a gallery experience without interrupting their studies.

Communication

The single most important job of a gallery owner is to communicate often and clearly with their artists.

- Send regular inventory lists.
- Send emails the very day merchandise is delivered to the gallery. (And say something nice! Such as, love the new work! Why? Because they have just spent hours and hours creating it and you are the first person who might be looking at it!)
- Send emails to let the artist know when you are returning work and why (for repair, to exchange so as to freshen stock, at their request, etc).

Agreements/contracts

An agreement is to clarify how you are going to work with the artist, what is expected of them, what they can be guaranteed from you. (See Addendum for a sample contract.) This is a subject that is still considered controversial is some arenas. We've had contracts for the last ten years. We wouldn't be without. Check with your attorney, and perhaps with your insurance company to determine if you will conduct business with or without a contract.

Payment

Because of the number of artists we represent, and

because paying is a demanding process, we have a pay period from the tenth of each month to the 10th of the next month. We cut the check and mail it on the thirtieth of that month. We also let the artist know if an item is on layaway and we pay them their wholesale amount when the item is paid in full.

Clarification

We ask each artist to always send paperwork with their merchandise. And we ask them to be clear about the price on their inventory sheet. We often use language like, "Is this the amount we will pay you when the item sells?" You would be surprised at how many young artists don't know the definition of Wholesale and Retail.

Publicity/advertising

Again, the contract states the artist's responsibility when it comes to advertising: they have to provide us with professional-quality photography. Without appropriate photographs they miss the opportunity to be chosen for print advertising. We pay for all advertising. From the very beginning of my business, I made the decision to control the ads that represent Facèré. If I'm in control, I pay.

How much should a gallery spend on advertising? The only suggestion I've seen was in a national jewelry magazine. Their suggestion was for 10% of gross sales for a boutique jewelry store (as close a definition to a jewelry art gallery that I have found). We've spent more and we've spent less. Our goal remains 10%.

Wear your jewelry. If you won't wear it, why would anyone else?

There have been occasions when artists have come to the gallery wearing his or her jewelry. Conversation ensues. They return to show a broader selection. Facèré has been known to print a contract then and there.

So, artists, wear your jewelry! Wherever you go. Perhaps it is not a gallery owner you wish to impress. Perhaps it is a potential customer you will impress. Never go anywhere without your jewelry!

Besides, if you don't wear the jewelry you make, why would anyone else? Wear jewelry when you go to the grocery store, church, class, bank…you get it. If you are in the business or thinking of getting into the business of selling art, you have to become your greatest advocate.

And, if you are reading this workbook to open a gallery of more than jewelry art, or other than jewelry art, here's advice:

- Paintings? Cover your walls.
- Fabric? Cover your body- Sculpture? Fill your yard – front and back.
- Jewelry? Never go without.

Gallery owner, who owns the merchandise?

You don't, unless you buy it. We have a gallery rule that if you wear jewelry art from the gallery, it is understood that you are giving serious consideration to buying it. You have one day to decide if the jewelry fits you in terms of style, weight, and ease of wearing. At the end of the day, you either buy it or put it back. The expectation is that you are trying on to buy, not trying on until the next day when you try on another piece.

Jewelry art defines who you are. If I'm wearing a piece of jewelry art, it's mine. I'm not wearing a piece to sell it to you. I'm wearing a piece of jewelry art to define who I am.

I believe it is not appropriate for gallery owners to wear jewelry art of their artists for the purpose of selling it. This belief came about when an artist friend who worked in fabrics told me of her distress:

"My gallery owner attended a major event. A society event. She wore one of my coats. She has never, ever purchased a piece of my work for herself. I'm pulling out of the gallery, I am so angry."

I took that story to heart. We, at Facèré, support our artists, just like our customers support our artists. It seems to me purchasing their work is one of the ways we honor the work we sell.

Giving jewelry a tryout

A word of advice to artists making jewelry. You need to give your work a trial run. Check for size, weight, (general comfort), versatility. This includes the men out there creating jewelry. If you can't or won't wear jewelry (which you should!), get a friend, spouse, significant other to be your wearing model. You need to know.

Artists, make your jewelry versatile

You owe it to yourself to study Victorian jewelry. It was not unusual that a tiara became a bracelet, became a necklace, and became a brooch. All in one piece.

Try to at least make a brooch that can be worn on a wire or on a chain as a necklace. You've doubled your market.

And everyone, wear jewelry art!

Yes, I already said that. It bears saying again.

WORKBOOK CHAPTER SEVENTEEN
THE CUSTOMER

Gifts

For the past ten years we have sent gifts to our best customers. The gift is sent with a 'thank-you' letter. The letter states, "This is a gift to say thank-you." Perhaps it sounds a bit simplistic, but there are times you need to say exactly what you are doing. Like giving a gift. Say thank-you for their support, interest, and loyalty. Make the gift memorable and appropriate. We started with cherry candies (for the pronunciation of the name of our gallery). Later we sent picture frames. Another year, the gift was a tube of word magnets (all relating to jewelry). The best part of this gift giving was that it led to our creation and giving of *Signs of Life*, the literary magazine we produce once a year.

Celebrations

Our biggest give-away is at our Holiday Ornament Give-away. Customers need to be present to win, and there is no question that we hope they are scouting out holiday gifts. But, with no-holds-barred, all the customers need to be included is to RSVP (and they are encouraged to bring guests). Names are put in a Facèré sack and we draw them during the party. The gifts?

Fabulous ornaments made by the artists. Ninety percent of all of those ornaments never see a tree. They almost immediately go on a body. We usually have between twenty-five and thirty ornaments to give away. We also have received gift certificates from the building management ($25) and gift certificates from ROAD, the men's store next to our location. The chances of winning are very high! Each artist receives $40 for his or her ornament...and, due to the generosity of our artists, the value of some of the ornaments has been as high as $1000.

We also serve a variety of chocolates, delicious cream puffs, and pour many a glass of champagne. It's a great party!

Services

We try to go the extra mile with our customers over repairs. If anything has happened to the piece of jewelry (not including running over it with a truck), we try to restore or repair any damage for up to a year. Sizing of rings we cover for the first size.

Repairs

Sometimes we go further than is warranted, which is my call as the owner. But we also protect ourselves by doing the following:

Whenever a customer brings in a diamond ring, and that diamond is a quarter carat or more, we plot the

Building A Business, Building A life

stone under the microscope. We plot the diamond for inclusions and any chips. Then the customer looks under the microscope and verifies that they have seen the identifying characteristics. This plotting of the stone is a must! We've heard too many scary stories about a diamond ring being brought to a jeweler who does not check it. Then, mysteriously, the diamond is returned and it isn't a diamond. Customers worry about this intrusion and dishonesty. Owners of shops who deal with diamonds need to protect themselves and at the same time assure the customer that you understand their concern about "switching" stones. Everyone knows a horror story—from both sides of the counter.

Facing the facts about the return

With a smile....well, at least, not a frown, we approach the return as an "opportunity." I do not say this lightly. Returns are horrible. But, returns happen. We try to make the best of it:

- Before you sell one item (your very first sale!), be sure your receipt states clearly:

Returns must be made within fourteen days of purchase. There is a ___% restocking fee for all returns. (You may wish to only apply this charge for cash and charge card refunds. Returns that result in another sale are often larger than the original sale.)

- Ask the customer to explain what isn't working with the gift. Get a conversation going.

- If you can detect that there is no hope of salvaging a sale (believe me, you'll recognize this almost immediately), make the return easy. Check the returned item for damage. Ask for the receipt. (Sometimes you'll even get the gift box back!) Ask the customer if he or she wishes to take a store credit or a refund (99% of the returnees, no matter how you've engaged them in conversation, know what they want). Try to save the sale with a store credit, but graciously be prepared to lose the sale.

- When there is hope, your job is to help the customer consider another purchase or a credit.

- Conduct the return quickly. Returns are not what you want your other customers seeing!

- Then forget about it. There will be another sale, another day.

The next idea

- Sometimes the chosen gift just isn't working: too big, too small, wrong color, wrong length, too heavy...but the recipient does not want to hurt the feelings of the gift giver. This customer needs your direction. Walk the gallery with the customer and make a "thinking tray" of all the possible exchanges. You are taking care of the situation and opening up choices.

- Check the past purchasing history of the customer to

learn what choices were previously made and were well received. This will help you help the customer. Show new work by the artist they've purchased in the past. Show work that is complimentary to what they have chosen before.

And listen!!

Listen carefully. Follow your customers lead. No posts? No dangling earrings? Needs classic? Needs to stay exactly in the budget of the returned item? If you are listenting carefully, you won't get ahead of your customer. Let the customer's ideas lead you. And then? You might come up with the perfect solution...because you listened.

The shifting budget

Your customer's budget is often fluid. Even though the customer states clearly that he or she wishes to spend $500, that customer may or may not mean it. Sometimes, all by himself, after he has carefully considered ten items for under $500, he chooses a $1000 item. I'm always surprised! I thought the customer truly had a limit. Remember the budget, but when you create the "thinking tray" include a couple of higher end items. Just in case.

WORKBOOK CHAPTER EIGHTEEN
RANT AND RAVE: THE CUSTOMERS

Customers come in all shapes, sizes, temperaments, spending ability, history, expectations, needs, past history. To create more raves than rants here are a few suggestions:

Remember names and if you don't remember, try one of the following:

- "Please forgive me. Tell me your first name." With such a question, you sound as if you've only forgotten half of the equation.

- Wait until you have the charge card in hand and immediately say, "(Name), I'll have that gift wrapped for you in just a minute."

- If he or she is there to pick up a special order or a repair, say, "Tell me your last name again." They'll think you certainly know their first name and once you have their last name, you will see the first name on the receipt.

- If you can get away with it, say, "I'm having a senior moment. I'm so embarrassed. Tell me your name." Save this as your very last "save" and it helps if you can

Building A Business, Building A life

touch their arm in the process (I'm not sure why that is the case, as it is a fawning gesture, but sometimes fawning saves the moment).

Offer to look up past purchases on the computer.

This is a particularly good move if you don't want a husband (sorry if that sounds sexist, but it usually is a husband), to give the very same gift he gave two years ago. Here's why: people are consistent. Men buying gifts, particularly. So check previous purchases and then ask, "Did she love the _____?" Any hesitation on his part might mean something like: the earrings were too long or too heavy, that she never wears brooches, that she loves classic and he purchased "edgy," etc. Or maybe he doesn't remember what he purchased, but if she didn't return the item, you can say, "Last time you purchased _____ (name of artist), and she just sent us a new selection, and _____ (name an article) would be a perfect match to the piece you gave her in August!" This tactic is well worth checking the computer for a selling/buying history. It also makes you look like you care!

Have another staff person check price tags when you are putting out new inventory.

There is nothing worse than looking at a price tag, and before you can stop yourself you say, "I can't believe this is the price!" Talk about a customer losing confidence!! There have been times when we sell an item at wholesale (wrong price on the tag), just to save face. Looking careless or stupid is not how to garner confidence from your customers.

Give your customer something with each purchase.

With every purchase we present the customer with a "packaged" resumé, artist statement, and any current printed material, e.g. newspaper article, magazine article about the artist or about Facèré. "Packaged" means it comes in its own large envelope with the gallery name and address. We also include in the packet a cover letter telling the customer why we have given him/her this information. For example, "You have entered the world of collecting jewelry art." That letter makes the assumption that the customer is now a collector. Making a customer a collector is our goal for every sale. A high ambition. Sometimes it is true!! We try to remember to remove the letter when the customer has purchased previously.

Spend time with small children and students.

Who knew that Facèré would be around long enough to serve the second generation? Those small children are now in college, getting married, buying Mother's Day presents. Facèré, in many instances has become the "family" jewelry source. Besides, watching small children become grown-ups keeps one humble.

Always, always treat each person (this includes those people asking the location of the restroom) as if they are a customer.

Building A Business, Building A life

Guess what? The potential is always there.

Insuring items left for repair.

Always indicate on the repair envelope, and on the "stub" of the envelope that you have given the customer, that their piece is insured for: _____. We are generous with this amount. It is also a reasonable amount. We ask the customer if they agree. If they say "yes," we both initial the stub and the repair envelope. Even though we have never lost a piece of jewelry in thirty-eight years, it doesn't mean we couldn't. Protect yourself! Protect your client. This is one of those very, "Do unto others..." moments. If you cannot agree on a reasonable amount for insurance, you might wish to send the customer on to a competitor.

Your gallery/shop/salon is your living room.

Treat customers as if they have just walked into your home. Your gallery or shop is in almost every way, your home! Greet the customer. If it is their first visit, tell him or her a little bit about your gallery. In our case we always explain that they are free to open the drawers to see more, and different, jewelry (as we say this, we open a drawer by way of explanation).

Learn when to leave your customer alone. Know when to return to your customer to show them an item. Don't ask if they need help. Don't ask anything that might require a "no" answer. Be engaging without being "pushy." Watch the best salesperson in your organization. Mimic them. "Best" means the person who is the most involved and who (hate to say this, but this is what you, behind the counter are there for) sells the most!

WORKBOOK CHAPTER NINETEEN
A SPECTACULAR STAFF

The staff is the glue that keeps Facèré in business. So, here is a final workbook page that stands on its own.

Playing well with others – Taking care of the staff

I've a staff of angels. At the present time, we five are all women (I've had men…and Jim Morgan…you were just the best!). I feel as if I work with the sisters I never had. We've been together from five to twenty-five years. Here are some things that keep us loving like sisters and not being crazy and angry like sisters:

Staff meetings

We have one-hour staff meetings every two months. We always have an agenda. Each person is expected to report on what their concerns are at the moment or to report on the project they have been assigned. Most often we use the staff meetings to plan events like shows and receptions. We meet at a local coffee shop (yes, it is a Starbucks!) and if the staff person has had to come to work on a day off, I pay two hours of work for one hour of meeting. I treat for the coffee. This hour away from the shop helps build good spirits. Everyone has an opportunity to speak. We discover problems to be solved. We laugh a lot.

Work schedule

Each of us has a different schedule and different requirements. Lorraine now has a dog that needs not to think she's deserted her. Susan has demands for her life as a calligrapher. Trudee is full time, but she needs to take a honeymoon soon. Mēgan often teaches and will be gone for many days depending on those opportunities. Dana takes time for beach living. I need time to write, to attend classes, and to fulfill board obligations. We always work hours out.

Pay and bonuses

No matter what, paydays are never missed. If I have to borrow from my line of credit, so be it. If I'm not at work on the first or the sixteenth of the month when pay checks are due, I'll come in to the gallery early to write pay checks. Along with paying artists on time, paying staff on time is sacrosanct.

Holiday bonuses are never missed, but they vary in size. The holiday party is always at the Fairmont's private room off the Georgian Room. Very spiffy. Very expensive. Very perfect. It is our one blow-out brunch before going to work on the first Sunday of December. Everyone must bring a present for everyone. No one is supposed to spend more than $5. We get the best presents!

Gifts

Birthdays are not missed. Susan is the genius of birthday bags full of a selection of gifts. She gathers. We supplement. We split the costs.

Travel

Anyone who travels is expected to bring back a gift for each staff member (under $5). Why? I can't remember why we started this tradition. But it's great. It's a way to keep us in mind of each other. It's a way of saying "thank-you" for the flexible schedule.

ADDENDUM:
WORKSHEETS

If you can use them, you are free to copy any of the following forms:

1. Daily Task Sheet
This sheet is used every day of the year. It reminds us of tasks not finished or tasks so small they are easily forgotten. It also reminds us of "Auto Pays," birthdays, jobs and repairs due, wedding dates with deliveries scheduled a good week before the event.

2. Packing Slip
We ship almost every day. This form is duplicated. One sheet to accompany the merchandise. One sheet to be kept in a binder in the gallery. This sheet has saved us from calamity many a time. We know the day we shipped. We know the value. We know the items in the box. If a delivery goes awry, we know how to track it.

3. Diamond Plotting Form
This form is used with the receipt of any diamond. We plot a single identifying characteristic of the stone. Now the customer is at ease. And we are covered!

4. Appraisal Form
This is for taking notes when we visit the gemologist.

It is a sound record of what we have been told. We use this worksheet as a source of information for formal appraisals.

5. Artist's Agreement
Over the years we have reduced the "legalese" of this contract. We have done this for clarity and brevity. We continue to refine the language and with some artists we have written in exceptions when requested and when we agreed. This agreement we hope clarifies the responsibilities of artists and gallery.

6. Special Order Form
We have many special orders. Special orders require the size, materials, date due, and any special arrangements. The possibilities of forgetting a detail are numerous. This form helps keep problems to a minimum.

Daily Task Sheet
July 27, 2011 ~ Wednesday

__ Check the Daily Task sheet from the previous day – complete assignments.
__ Check the calendar for appointments scheduled for today and tomorrow.
__ Make the bank deposit.
__ Check the emails: respond, print out, and file.
__ Check the repair files for work that needs to go out to a vendor or be picked up.
__ Check 'To be Mailed' and 'Hold' files and process.
__ Check the Special Order Book: call artists and/or customers if necessary.
__ Restock Artist biography materials for handouts.
__ Check gallery displays: organize and replenish items.
__ Read the phone log and respond to requests.
__ Recheck the layaway invoices and final payments from the previous day.
__ Check tags on artwork: refresh if necessary.
__ Check ring handout cards: refresh if necessary.
__ Process sold items on website.

Packing Slip

Date_____ Packed by_____
How Shipped _____

Shipped To:
_____
_____
_____

Telephone: _____

Email: _____

Artist	Description	Retail Price

Notes:

Please notify us: 206-624-6768 or at facereart@aol.com (mailto:facereart@aol.com) if there are any questions or concerns!

Facèré Jewelry Art Gallery
 1420 Fifth Avenue, Suite 108, Seattle, WA 98101

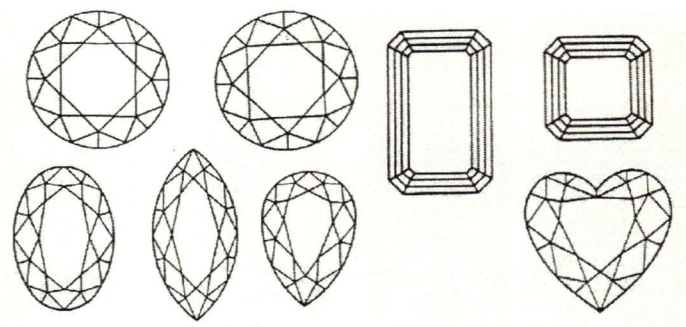

Facèré Jewelry Art Gallery, Inc.

{ } This stone is being plotted for identification purposes only. **One** distinctive feature has been plotted. Not all flaws or characteristics are shown.

{ } In this quick analysis, no inclusions are apparent at 10 power magnification. *(This does not indicate a complete absence of inclusions.)*

Stones look different when clean.

I verify that I have left my stone with Facèré and I agree to the identification.

Facèré has taken in a colorless faceted stone, insured for $_____, while in our care.

Customer Signature _____

Employee _____

Date Left _____

~~~~~~~~~~~~~~~~~~~~~~~~~~~~~~~~

I verify that my stone was returned on _____

Customer Signature _____

Employee _____

Facèré Jewelry Art Gallery
Appraisal Form

Date_____ Item # _____

Appraiser _____

_____

Customer _____
Address _____

_____

Telephone _____
Email _____

Item Description _____

_____

Metals _____
Weight _____

Stones _____
Weight _____ Size _____ Color _____
Clarity _____ Cut _____
Other Materials _____
Measurements _____

Makers Marks _____

Value for Insurance _____
Value for Retail Sale _____

Employee who took verbal information _____
Employee who prepared Appraisal _____

Stone Plotted: Yes_____ No _____

Additional Notes/Comments: _____

_____
_____

Appraisal: Picked up by Customer _____
           Mailed _____
           Date _____

SHOW TITLE

Dates of Show: Wednesday, XXXXXXXX
Opening: Wednesday, XXXXXXXX
Lecture: 4:00 (RSVP 206-624-6768 – limited seating)
Reception: 5:00 – 7:00 pm

Number of items for show: XX items
Work due: XXXXXXXX

THIS AGREEMENT IS BETWEEN:
Facèrè International, Inc.
dba Facèrè Jewelry Art Gallery
1420 5TH AVENUE #108
SEATTLE, WA 98101
206-624-6768 / fax: 206-624-2852
Email: facereart@aol.com

AND JEWELRY ARTIST:

_____

Artist Name; as it should appear in print.

_____
_____

Address

_____

Telephone

_____

Email

A. TERM

1. The term of this Agreement is for the period running from. XXXXXXXX The return of unsold jewelry, no later than XXXXXXXX.

2. Any sales of jewelry displayed in this show to anyone living in the State of Washington will be considered a sale of Facèré Jewelry Art Gallery through 30 days beyond the final day of the show.

B. EXCLUSIVITY

1. During the term of this Agreement, while work is on display, Facèré Jewelry Art Gallery shall represent the work in this show as the Jewelry Artist's sole and exclusive agent in the State of Washington.

2. If the artist is represented by another gallery in the State of Washington, signage will accompany the work: *(Artist's name) represented by* _____. There is no financial obligation with such gallery.

C. SALES AND PAYMENT

1. <u>All work must be for sale.</u>

2. Jewelry Artist shall provide Facèré Jewelry Art Gallery with no less than XXXXXXXX pieces of jewelry for display during the term of this Agreement, unless an alternative number of items is first agreed to by both the Jewelry Artist and an authorized representative of Facèré Jewelry Art Gallery.

3. The initial wholesale price of each item of the Jewelry Artist's jewelry will be determined solely by the Jewelry Artist and will be the minimum price for the purpose of this Agreement. The Artist will be paid the designated wholesale price following the sale of jewelry through Facèré Jewelry Art Gallery, in accordance with the terms of this Agreement. The Artist shall identify the wholesale price of each piece of jewelry on a dated invoice with a full description of the item. No sales of the Jewelry Artist's jewelry shall occur until the Jewelry

Artist's designated written wholesale price for the piece of jewelry is received by Facèré Jewelry Art Gallery, and a retail price is determined by Facèré Jewelry Art Gallery for the jewelry.

4. Facèré Jewelry Art Gallery shall be entitled to establish a retail price of 2.15 times the wholesale price. Facèré Jewelry Art Gallery's decision to sell at a discount shall not alter Facèré Jewelry Art Gallery's obligation to pay the full designated wholesale price to the Jewelry Artist, as stated in paragraph C-3 of this Agreement.

5. Payment to the Jewelry Artist for items sold will be made within 20 days of the close of the show by check or Paypal. Payment by any other method, as requested by the artist, will be at the expense of the artist (i.e. wire transfer).

6. Should Facèré Jewelry Art Gallery accept a return after the show for which the Jewelry Artist has already been paid the Jewelry Artist's wholesale price, the returned item shall be considered wholly owned by Facèré Jewelry Art Gallery, the Jewelry Artist shall have no repayment obligation to Facèré Jewelry Art Gallery and shall be entitled to no payment upon future sale of the piece.

7. Jewelry Artist shall pay for shipping work to Facèré Jewelry Art Gallery. Facèré Jewelry Art Gallery shall pay for USPS Priority return shipping of works to the Jewelry Artist. Any costs related to express/overnight shipping or otherwise special handling requested by the Jewelry Artist will be the responsibility of the Artist and therefore not covered by Facèré Jewelry Art Gallery.

8. The Jewelry Artist shall not be entitled to remove jewelry from Facèré Jewelry Art Gallery for the

purpose of private sales during the terms of this agreement. If a customer, having seen a particular piece of work at the gallery, contacts the Jewelry Artist directly, either to purchase said piece or to contract with the Jewelry Artist to make a similar piece, the Jewelry Artist shall refer the customer to Facèré Jewelry Art Gallery and conduct any sale only through Facèré Jewelry Art Gallery, consistent with this Agreement.

9. The Jewelry Artist will receive a 10% discount on any purchase at Facèré Jewelry Art Gallery of regular priced items for Jewelry Artist's own use or for the Jewelry Artist to give as a gift during the time of this agreement.

D. PUBLICITY

1. Facèré Jewelry Art Gallery will be responsible for the costs of advertising for Facèré Jewelry Art Gallery during the duration of this contract. Facèré Jewelry Art Gallery reserves the sole right to choose which artists to feature in its advertising and does not guarantee that the Jewelry Artist will be featured in Facèré Jewelry Art Gallery's advertising. Facèré Jewelry Art Gallery will attempt to equably distribute the advertising opportunities between all of the artists in this show.

2. Facèré Jewelry Art Gallery currently maintains a website (facerejewelryart.com). The Jewelry Artists in this show will not be listed under 'Artists' on the website maintained by Facèré Jewelry Art Gallery. The show will be mentioned on the home page and under exhibits. Appropriate images from the Jewelry Artist in the show will be posted at the gallery's discretion.

3. The Jewelry Artist shall supply professional quality, digital images of the exact items to be in the show on a CD for advertising and other marketing purposes. The images can be in TIF or JPG format, and must be two

megabyte (4x6 inches at 300ppi) *minimum*. By signing this agreement, the Jewelry Artist authorizes Facèrè Jewelry Art Gallery to use such images and warrants that no permission from any third party need be obtained by Facèrè Jewelry Art Gallery in advance of such use. If photo credit is requested, the Jewelry Artist shall notify Facèrè Jewelry Art Gallery of such a request in a timely manner. Facèrè Jewelry Art Gallery will attempt to include such photo credit in advertising.

4. The Jewelry Artist shall provide Facèrè Jewelry Art Gallery with a current resumé of her or his work and an accompanying Artist's statement. The Jewelry Artist is encouraged to send these pieces of information electronically. The Jewelry Artist authorizes these materials to be reproduced by Facèrè Jewelry Art Gallery or others on Facèrè Jewelry Art Gallery's behalf, in whole or part.

5. Artist consents to the display of the Jewelry Artist's jewelry or images of the Artist's jewelry by Facèrè Jewelry Art Gallery in any manner deemed appropriate by Facèrè Jewelry Art Gallery.

E. INSURANCE / CARE OF MERCHANDISE / MISCELLANEOUS

1. The Jewelry Artist shall be responsible for all costs of insurance required to insure the Jewelry Artist's jewelry before Facèrè Jewelry Art Gallery takes possession of the jewelry. Facèrè Jewelry Art Gallery shall have no liability for any loss or damage to the Jewelry Artist's jewelry before Facèrè Jewelry Art Gallery takes possession of the jewelry. Once Facèrè Jewelry Art Gallery takes possession of the jewelry, Facèrè Jewelry Art Gallery will insure all jewelry of the Jewelry Artist in its possession against loss of or damage to the jewelry for the wholesale price of the jewelry designated by

the Artist as set forth above, and will also maintain umbrella liability insurance against third party claims in the amount of $1,000,000. Facèré Jewelry Art Gallery will further provide insurance against loss of or damage to the jewelry for the wholesale price of the jewelry during its transfer back to the Jewelry Artist. Insurance does not cover 'Acts of God' or terrorist attacks. Once the jewelry is in the Jewelry Artist's possession, Facèré Jewelry Art Gallery shall have no further obligation for the returned jewelry.

2. Facèré Jewelry Art Gallery will make every effort to keep the Jewelry Artist's work clean and properly maintained while it is in Facèré Jewelry Art Gallery's possession.

3. If an item of jewelry is damaged while in the care of Facèré Jewelry Art Gallery and the damage is not repairable by the Jewelry Artist, the item will be purchased by Facèré Jewelry Art Gallery at the wholesale price. Such item will then be wholly owned by Facèré Jewelry Art Gallery.

4. All work submitted to Facèré Jewelry Art Gallery must include a description of all materials used, and carat weight of precious stones. When gold, silver, or titanium are used, identification of metal and karat will appear on the work.

5. This Agreement shall be governed by Washington State law. In the event any portion of this Agreement shall be determined to be unenforceable, the enforceability of the remainder of this Agreement shall not be affected and shall continue in full force and effect. This Agreement represents the sole and entire Agreement of the parties and supersedes any prior agreements, negotiations or discussions between them. No alteration or modification of any of the provisions

of this Agreement shall be valid unless made in writing and signed by both parties.

6. This contract is a privileged and private agreement between the Jewelry Artist and Facèré Jewelry Art Gallery.

_____
Jewelry Artist

_____
Facèré International Inc, dba Facèré Jewelry Art Gallery./Karen Lorene, Owner

Date _____

Facèré Jewelry Art Gallery - SPECIAL ORDER

Artist _____

Artist confirmation date: _____

Customer Name: _____
Phone: _____
Email: _____
Address: _____

Special Order Instructions:

_____
_____

Design Area:

Communication Log:

_____ _____
_____ _____
_____ _____
_____ _____
_____ _____
_____ _____

Estimates:
    Date: _____ $ _____
    Date: _____ $ _____

Go Ahead!
Date: _____ $ _____ Item # _____

Due Date: _____ **Date Completed:** _____